PASCAL'S PHILOSOPHY
OF RELIGION

PASCAL'S PHILOSOPHY
OF RELIGION

BY

CLEMENT C. J. WEBB

Oriel Professor of Philosophy of the
Christian Religion in the
University of Oxford

OXFORD

AT THE CLARENDON PRESS

1929

KRAUS REPRINT CO.
New York
1970

OXFORD UNIVERSITY PRESS
AMEN HOUSE, E.C. 4
LONDON EDINBURGH GLASGOW
LEIPZIG NEW YORK TORONTO
MELBOURNE CAPETOWN BOMBAY
CALCUTTA MADRAS SHANGHAI
HUMPHREY MILFORD
PUBLISHER TO THE
UNIVERSITY

LC 30-8112

Reprinted with the permission of the Licensor
KRAUS REPRINT CO.
A U.S. Division of Kraus-Thomson Organization Limited

Printed in U.S.A.

PREFACE

THIS study, not of Pascal, but of his contribution to what we now call the Philosophy of Religion, contains the substance of a course of lectures delivered in the Michaelmas Term of 1926. They are published not without hesitation, as perhaps one should only choose for detailed discussion those great men who have evoked in one's own soul a special sympathy or from whom one has been able to learn most; and Pascal is not to me especially sympathetic, nor is he a teacher to whom I feel myself under a peculiar obligation. But the fact that he is a thinker whom some historians of philosophy almost ignore, while others exalt him to the highest rank among those who have handled the profoundest problems of human nature and human destiny, may make an attempt to estimate his true position in this respect not uninteresting to students of the Philosophy of Religion, and as such an attempt I offer this little work to their consideration.

The references to Pascal's writings in the footnotes are, when not otherwise stated, to M. Léon Brunschvicg's convenient edition of the *Pensées et Opuscules*, published by Hachette.

C. C. J. W.

CONTENTS

I

INTRODUCTION

IT is said, and said truly up to a certain point, that
Science and Philosophy know nothing of national
divisions. Of Science indeed, in the restricted sense
in which we now commonly use that term, the statement falls very little short of being entirely true; for
Science, abstracting as it does altogether from all
but certain aspects of the reality with which we are
conversant in experience, so far as it concerns itself
at all with the mind of the observer of the object
which it studies, is interested only in those characteristics which are common to all men, at any rate
at a certain level of culture, and not with those in
which national differences make their appearance. It
is less true as regards Philosophy, because Philosophy aims at a complete comprehension of reality,
a complete account of experience; and it is impossible to deny that national differences do exist, and
do affect the way in which individuals of various
nationalities apprehend the world. But Philosophy
also, though not moving like Science in a region
where national differences are all but wholly irrele-
vant, is bound to transcend those differences, and
to take account of them only as they contribute to,
and distract or enrich, the one life of rational mind
or Spirit which it endeavours to mirror or describe.
Hence we expect to find an agreement among nations

embraced within the same system of civilized society as to the place occupied in the development of thought by those who have individually made the greatest contributions to it. No doubt one is not surprised that, since to most men their mother tongue is more familiar than any other, the philosophers who write in a particular language will be also commonly more familiar to those whose native tongue it is than philosophers who have used a different idiom; but, although an intimate acquaintance with Locke and Berkeley may more naturally be looked for in an English student of philosophy than in a French, and, conversely, acquaintance with Descartes and Malebranche in a French than in an English student, we expect to find in standard histories of philosophy, in whichever tongue they may be written, a full recognition of the importance and significance of both pairs of thinkers. Nevertheless, it is true that there are certain cases in which a remarkable difference of estimate, and not merely of familiarity, may reveal itself between different nations in respect of individual philosophers; and to two of these I wish to call attention: they are those of an Englishman, Francis Bacon, and a Frenchman, Blaise Pascal.

A hundred years ago—even sixty or seventy years ago—it was traditional in this country to regard Francis Bacon as one of the very greatest of all philosophers. When Tennyson in his *Palace of Art* transferred to him the celebrated title which Dante had devised for Aristotle and spoke of 'Plato the wise and large-browed Verulam, The first of those who know', he was expressing himself in entire accordance with the common view of educated Englishmen in his day. They might not all have subscribed to the extravagance of Macaulay's essay, which exalted Bacon above the ancients on grounds which he would himself have been far from approving, but they would generally have admitted his claim to stand with Plato and Aristotle in the foremost rank of those who have devoted themselves, in the Platonic phrase, to the survey of all time and all existence. Yet even then historians of philosophy in other countries, while not denying to him a place in the succession of such, were not accustomed to follow his fellow countrymen in rating him with the highest. He was for them rather an interesting and influential figure of the period of transition from the medieval to the modern period of thought, or at the most a distinguished pioneer of one of the principal schools of modern thought, than one of the two or three supreme philosophers of all time. Yet in the year 1926, in which was celebrated the tercentenary of his death, it was at one time quite doubtful whether the British Academy could find any outstanding philosopher prepared to make his *éloge* as a philosopher[1]; so strangely had the old English tradition respecting him, to which Tennyson's lines quoted

---

[1] The task was eventually consigned to the competent hands of Professor A. E. Taylor.

above give expression, died out, within my own memory, among professional students of philosophy.

I have said this much of Bacon because I think we may draw an instructive parallel between him and Pascal, to whom I am preparing to devote this course of lectures, in respect of the difference between the estimate of them usual among their own countrymen and that which we find outside their own nation. The two men are themselves extremely dissimilar; and that is indeed what one would expect from the very fact that each is so pre-eminently representative of his own people that it has in either case caused a singular divergence between the estimate of them formed by their compatriots and that formed by those who stand outside the national tradition for which they are pre-eminent.

No one questions that Pascal was a great man of science; and, although not every one who reads him will be equally attracted and impressed by the type of piety to which his writings on religion give expression, no one would, I think, be disposed to deny him a distinguished place among Christian apologists. But while it would be quite easy to find histories of philosophy, English or German, which take no account of him at all, for Frenchmen he is, and remains—for there has, I think, been no such abandonment of the high claim made on his behalf by national tradition as has happened in England in respect of Bacon (rather perhaps the reverse) a great philosopher, among the very greatest. Professor

Jacques Chevalier's recent book upon him is a proof of this. Not only does Professor Chevalier assert (and here a foreigner has no right to contradict him) that Pascal is the man most representative of the genius of his race—that he is to France what Plato is to Greece, Dante to Italy, Cervantes or St. Theresa to Spain, Shakespeare to England—but that Descartes and he are the two giants of modern thought—our Plato and our Aristotle. The noteworthy religious and Catholic revival within the last few years among French scholars and students of philosophy has been intimately associated with a renewed interest in and study of Pascal, that is of the Pascal of the *Pensées*, in whose unfinished defence of Christianity—and more particularly of Roman Catholic Christianity—they find a quality which in their judgement enables it to appeal to the hearts and minds of men bred in an intellectual atmosphere as different as is that of the twentieth from that of the seventeenth century.

I will here make the confession that I cannot myself, for reasons which will appear as this book proceeds, regard Pascal as in the strict sense a philosopher—in the sense in which among Frenchmen Descartes, Malebranche, Bergson are philosophers —at all. He was a man of science and he was also a saint, who had this indeed of the philosopher about him, that he was not able, as some religious men of

[1] Published by Hachette, 1922, in the series of *Les Grands Philosophes*—a pendant to his earlier work in the same series about Descartes (1921).

science have found themselves able, to keep his science and his religion in separate compartments of his life, but thought about their relationship to one another and felt the need of a unified view of the world. But he was able to acquiesce in a view which, as I shall contend, was not, properly speaking, a philosophical one. It is significant that the two men whose reflexions on life, as his *Entretien avec M. de Saci* shows, had made the greatest impression upon him were Epictetus and Montaigne—neither of them philosophers, we may say, in what we now regard as the strict sense of the word; though the former no doubt surveyed life from the standpoint of a philosophical system which he accepted, much as men at a later date accepted a theology supposed to be authoritatively revealed, as supplying a framework for his reflexions. Bacon and Pascal were both great men; they both became specially dear to their countrymen, whose language they had wielded with the power of genius, and both reflected deeply and widely on life. It is therefore not unnatural that appreciation of their real greatness should have sometimes obscured the fact that they had not that primary interest in speculation on the ultimate structure of reality, for the mere sake of knowing what it is, which we nowadays take to be the peculiar qualification of the philosopher in the strict and proper sense of the word.

II

PASCAL AND THE THOUGHT OF HIS AGE

IT will be convenient here to enumerate the more important dates in Pascal's short life. He was born at Clermont in Auvergne in 1623. He was twelve years old when, in 1635, his mathematical genius discovered itself on the famous occasion when his father, who had forborne to teach him or allow him to study any mathematics, found that he had in secret, calling circles 'rounds' and lines 'bars', progressed so far in geometry as to discover by himself the proof of Euclid i. 32—of the proposition, that is, that the sum of the angles of a triangle is always equal to two right angles. At the age of eighteen he invented an 'arithmetical machine'; at the age of twenty-three he made the celebrated experiment which, confirming those of Torricelli, established that the phenomena once attributed to nature's horror of a vacuum are to be explained by the pressure of the atmosphere. It was in the same year, 1646, that Pascal with the rest of his family experienced what has been called his 'first conversion' —a serious impression of the supreme importance of religion, brought about by his introduction, through two gentlemen who were staying in his father's house and who were disciples of Saint-Cyran, the director of the nuns of Port-Royal, to the movement which has gone by the name of Jansenism.

This 'first conversion' may thus be called a conversion to Jansenism, or rather to the austere piety associated with Saint-Cyran and Port-Royal, and which had as its intellectual background the *Augustinus* of Jansen, Bishop of Ypres, whose friend Saint-Cyran had been. In this book the author had attempted to revive Augustine's doctrine of justification, with its emphasis on divine predestination and on the incapacity of the human will since the fall to obey the commandments of God except so far as it is determined wholly by the divine grace, in opposition to the doctrines of the contemporary Jesuit theologians, who were disposed to allow a larger part to man's own will in the work of his salvation and even, in the extreme form advocated by the Spaniard Molina, to reduce God's share in man's good actions to an original supply of 'sufficient grace' and a subsequent 'simultaneous concourse' with the man's own free will. I shall have to speak again of Pascal's concern in these controversies about Grace, and am at present only noting as an epoch in his life his adoption of the principles of the school of earnestly religious men who set their faces against the laxity of theory and practice which, as it seemed to them, the powerful Jesuit order was encouraging and, through the wide extent of its activities in the confessional, encouraging all too successfully. In 1651 Pascal's father died; and Pascal appears for some time afterwards to have entered more than he had done before, or was to do later, into the pleasures of social life.

Although, as it would appear, he never lapsed either into disbelief of Christianity or into a course of life that would be commonly reckoned as immoral, there is no doubt that at this period he lived in the world, and that between his scientific researches and his social engagements religion ceased to be the chief preoccupation of his life. But three years later, in 1654, he underwent what is usually described as his 'definitive conversion'; and after that, religion became the chief preoccupation of his life and continued so until the end. In 1656 he began his famous *Lettres Provinciales* against the Jesuits, and in 1662 he died at the early age of 39, leaving behind him only fragments of his intended Apology for Christianity in the form of what are known as his *Pensées*, or Thoughts.

Our discussion of his Philosophy of Religion will be in the main based upon these *Pensées*; but it will include some consideration of the attitude revealed in his *Lettres Provinciales* towards the problems of sin and grace, in the contemporary controversy about which he took so important a part.

It will be convenient in the first place to set Pascal's philosophy of religion against the background of the general history of thought upon the subject. But in so doing it is important to note that Pascal was anything but learned in philosophical or even in theological literature. Speaking of his early education, the late M. Boutroux, in his little book on Pascal, says with, I think, substantial truth that 'his education in theology must have been extremely elementary. When he comes to attack this science he will have everything to learn and will never have more than a schoolboy's proficiency in it. Even in philosophy he acquired no more than some very general notions at the time of his studies with his father. The small learning which he will hereafter possess in that department he will owe to some later reading.' [1]

It is, no doubt, true that neither in philosophy nor in theology can the importance of the contribution made by a man of original genius be measured by the extent of his acquaintance with its literature. Some of the greatest thinkers whom the world has seen have been in no sense learned scholars in philosophical literature. But in regard to Pascal it may, I think, be said that he was not merely ill-equipped in philosophical and theological erudition; he was not really deeply interested in theological problems for their own sake; while he can scarcely be said to have envisaged the problem of philosophy as a subject of inquiry on its own account at all. He was, as I said before, a man of science and a saint; and the question of the relative importance of his scientific researches and his religious experiences, and of the bearing on the latter of the spectacle of human life, as presented to the view of an educated man of his day, engaged his most serious attention. But while as a man of science and as a religious man he speaks as one who knows at first hand what he

[1] Boutroux, *Pascal* (Par. 1900), p. 15.

is talking about, he moves in the sphere of philosophical and theological speculation as one who is rather an intelligent critic of what he finds those saying who are counted authorities therein than as concerned to originate speculations for himself, or as even primarily interested in the questions there discussed, apart from their bearing on our conduct and our expectations.

Pascal grew up in the lifetime of Descartes; and before he had attained his majority that great thinker, whom there is now a general agreement in regarding as the inaugurator of modern philosophy, had already published his principal works, and by them profoundly affected the whole intellectual outlook of the educated public in his own country and in western Europe generally. There was much in the philosophy of Descartes calculated to attract and engage the adhesion of such a man as Pascal. Both were mathematicians and found their philosophical ideal in the 'clear and distinct' ideas, as Descartes himself called them, which are characteristic of mathematical thought. Both on the other hand were convinced theists, and as loyal sons of the Church of France not merely theists but Christians and Roman Catholic Christians. It is no doubt true that religion was not for Descartes, as it was for Pascal, the chief preoccupation of his life, and it was, as we shall see, the difference between them in respect of religious experience, that at the end sets Pascal farther from Descartes than one would at first expect to find him.

But at present I wish rather to dwell upon what is common to the outlook of the elder and that of the younger thinker.

It was a consequence of the very slightness of Pascal's acquaintance with philosophical literature in general that no predilection for classical antiquity or for medieval scholasticism hindered his acquiescence in the general intellectual habits of his country and age; and these were unquestionably deeply penetrated by the spirit of Descartes. Let me mention two or three characteristics of the thought of the time which reflect, or perhaps one should say reflect themselves in, the work of Descartes, and which Pascal shared with his contemporaries. There is the desire to approach the facts of experience afresh, to doubt—or rather to call into question— with Descartes in the *Discours de la Méthode* all that can be doubted or questioned till one comes to something indubitable, such as Descartes himself declares for any thinker the thinker's own existence to be. Closely connected with this is a certain impatience of any reference to the authority of tradition in philosophy and a consequent depreciation of the value of erudition. This was in part no doubt a very intelligible reaction from a feature shared by medieval scholasticism with the philosophical reflection of the Renaissance period which had succeeded to it. Scholasticism, though in form perhaps more than in substance, was perpetually appealing to the authority of Aristotle in justifica-

tion of its arguments and conclusions; and the age
of the Renaissance, despite the revolt against the
tyranny of Aristotle which was in fashion among
its literary representatives, was characterized by an
attitude of veneration for and dependence upon
classical antiquity which tended to connect or even
to confuse erudition with philosophy, as it had
certainly not been confused or even connected in the
work of the great Schoolmen. The mathematical
sciences, from their highly abstract character and the
intuitive certainty—the 'clearness and distinctness'
—of the ideas in which they deal, are of all others
those for which tradition and erudition have least
importance; and thus a period in which these
sciences had as it were a new birth and were occupying the attention of the best minds of the age was
bound to be affected by the ideal which they suggest
of a truth attainable by each individual who chooses
to look and think for himself without prejudice or
arrière-pensée. Descartes' own work focused and encouraged this tendency to adopt such an ideal; it is
difficult indeed to acquit him in the pursuit of it of a
certain wilfulness in putting out of his own mind
and taking care not to suggest to the minds of others
his own actual debt to the books he had studied in
his youth. In the case of St. Augustine, in whom
may be found the germs of some of his most distinctive thoughts—for example, of the cogito ergo
sum and of the so-called ontological argument for
the existence of God—this has often been recognized.

M. Etienne Gilson[1] and Dr. Koyre[2] have recently
pointed out that it must be acknowledged in respect
of some of the great medieval Schoolmen also. But
if Pascal was, in respect of this mathematical ideal of
philosophy and of the revulsion from an over-
valuation of tradition and erudition which went with
it, a true son of the Cartesian age in which he grew
up, in respect of religion his relation to Descartes
was more ambiguous; and in point of fact the pro-
gress of his thought on this subject—and it is of
course with that that we are especially here concerned—tended to remove him farther from the
position of the elder thinker than he probably was
at first. For there were certain features of Descartes'
philosophy which must have recommended it to
the religious soul of Pascal. Consistently or not,
Descartes combined with a thoroughgoing mechanism in the explanation of material nature, including
therein the human organism, a not less thoroughgoing spiritualism in his account of *thought*. The existence of God was for him the presupposition and
guarantee of all our own thinking: the human spirit
was absolutely inexplicable by the mechanical principles which served for the explanation of the associated bodily organism, so that only by reference to the
divine Creator of both could his school ultimately
explain the actual co-operation of the two at every
moment of our lives. Pascal's view, which we shall

---

[1] *Études de Philosophie Médiévale* (Strasb. 1921), pp. 146 ff.
[2] *Descartes u. die Scholastik* (Bonn 1923).

afterwards have to discuss, of the relation between the *esprit*, which needs to be persuaded of the truth of religion, and the *automate*, which needs to be accustomed and habituated to behave as religion directs, has as its background, without precisely reproducing, the Cartesian dualism of soul and body. But, while Descartes was disposed to insist on the clear evidence of God's existence yielded by the very nature of our thought as establishing the foundations of a religious view of the world in the same region of intuitive certainty as those in which were established the foundations of the mathematical sciences, Pascal moved away from any such confidence in human reason to attain to the knowledge of God, and eventually, as we shall see, reached a position very remote from the Cartesian—a position which denied practically all value to any knowledge of God but that which came through his revelation of himself in Jesus Christ.

Pascal, however, is in respect of his attitude toward that revelation itself not very far from the personal position of Descartes, although undoubtedly his Christian experience was of a far intenser and more dominating character than any which we can suppose in the case of Descartes. For Descartes' attitude towards the religious tradition of his country was one which was characteristic of many of the representative figures both of the age to which he belonged and of that which had immediately preceded. Of this preceding age the outstanding event had been the ecclesiastical revolt of a large part of Europe from the allegiance of the Roman See, and the consequent disruption of the spiritual unity of western Christendom. The Reformers had found themselves enabled to accomplish this revolt by means of an appeal to Scripture; and their rejection of the authority of the ecclesiastical tradition and of the ecclesiastical hierarchy which had interpreted Scripture to preceding generations left the text of Scripture itself for them in a position not so much of greater authority as of a more isolated authority than it had previously enjoyed. With them there-fore there went hand in hand a revolt against one authority and an increased insistence upon another. The theological speculations of the Schoolmen, in which they had freely used the philosophy of Aristotle as a guide in the study of divine things, were disparaged at once for their reliance upon 'the Philosopher' and for their venturesomeness in passing, under his guidance, beyond the limits pre-scribed by the divine oracles. The Reformation was by no means in all its aspects a movement towards freedom of thought; in general it rather tended to limit liberty of speculation in the interests of sim-plicity than to promote it. I think it is true to say that the beginnings of the theory of development or evolution in doctrine, when they began to show themselves, are found rather in connexion with Catholicism than with orthodox Protestantism. Now neither Descartes nor Pascal were sons of the Reformation; but they were sons of the so-called Counter-Reformation. That movement was directed towards checking the centrifugal process which had already severed so much of the religious life of Europe from the communion of the Roman See, and therefore aimed at the adoption within that communion of whatever the spirit of the age seemed justifiably to demand, so far as that could be done without further schism. Thus it not only brought about a moral and doctrinal reform which delivered the Church in communion with Rome from the most glaring abuses and superstitions which had alienated so many of the best Christians of an earlier generation, but it also sought to effect a retreat upon the essentials of Christianity such as had been attempted by the Reformers; only it did not isolate Scripture as they had done from the ecclesiastical tradition of which it was the most venerable and authoritative part, but retained that tradition as its interpreter, and even as to some extent co-ordinate with it. This might at first sight seem to be all to the good; but in point of fact it tended to stereotype a much larger body of doctrine, and so to leave the mind considerably less freedom of expatiation and criticism than in the Churches of the Reformation. But what I am here mainly concerned to point out is that the attitude which had been hitherto associated with the Reformation—that of combining emphasis on freedom from all secular authority in scientific thought with emphasis (often in the interest of that very freedom),

on the authority of Scripture in its own sphere, on
which philosophy must not trespass, was reproduced
in the Church of the Counter-Reformation; except
that Scripture did not here stand alone, but was
combined with the teaching of the Fathers of the
primitive Church and the dogmatic decisions of the
Church in all ages as authoritative exponents of its
meaning. I am not of course pretending that this
distinction of spheres was a new thing; it remounts
at least to St. Thomas Aquinas; but it was intensified
and stereotyped in both branches of the western
Church as a result of the movement whereof both
the Protestant Reformation and the Catholic Counter-
Reformation are parts.

Now both Descartes and Pascal were in sympathy
with this difference of attitude towards authority in
secular science or philosophy and authority in theology. Both were as ready to admit authority in the
latter as they were indisposed to admit it in the
former, and Pascal expressly remarks on the perver-
sity of those who behave 'as if the respect which one
has for the ancient philosophers were a matter of
duty while that which one has for the most ancient
of the Fathers of the Church were no more than a
piece of good manners (*une bienséance*[1]).' But this
attitude was rendered easy for both because neither
(on the whole) was greatly interested in theology as
a science; and it is noticeable that it was precisely
where certain special circumstances awakened Pascal's

---

[1] *Fragment d'un Traité du Vide*, p. 77.

interest in a particular theological controversy—that about the nature of Grace—that he became at once less indifferent to theological subtleties and less submissive to theological authority than was the case in other departments.

Pascal thus had much in common with Descartes, and, indeed, was no doubt much affected by the influence of the elder philosopher, which pervaded, as I have said, the intellectual atmosphere in which he grew up. But there are indications that he became less Cartesian in his maturer years. It is perhaps unnecessary to deny all part in this change to the somewhat unsympathetic attitude which Descartes himself manifested toward an aspirant to scientific distinction so much his junior. When shown by Mersenne, the Jesuit father who was the friend and correspondent of all the most eminent thinkers in Europe of his time, of Hobbes and Gassendi as well as of Descartes, a mathematical essay of the sixteen-year-old Pascal, he refused to see in it anything but a clever pupil's reproduction of a master's teaching; and at a later date he persuaded himself that the famous experiment of the Puy-de-Dôme, when Pascal ascended that mountain and showed by experiment that mercury would rise higher in a tube at its top than at its bottom owing to the pressure of the atmosphere being less, was actually suggested to Pascal by himself; whereas Pascal was not at all conscious of having been indebted to him in this respect, though he must no doubt have been aware that his experiment was confirmatory of anticipations which Descartes had entertained. But, though Descartes' unsympathetic and even ungenerous attitude towards him personally might naturally tend to diminish Pascal's earlier enthusiasm for him, the real cause of dissatisfaction lay deeper. Descartes was no doubt a theist, a Christian, and a Roman Catholic; but he was a theist on the grounds of a philosophical argument, which he held should be found convincing by every unprejudiced mind which could follow it, independently of any specifically religious experience; and, although he was a devout Roman Catholic Christian, who vowed and performed a pilgrimage to Loretto on the occasion of his success in discovering a new philosophical method, his Christianity has the appearance of being based rather on his resolve to follow in these matters the religious tradition of his country than on any personal realization of its sole adequacy to meet the demands of his soul, such as convinced Pascal that it alone was the true religion. For Pascal, apart from the specifically religious and indeed specifically Christian experience of an inherent contradiction in human life which could find its solution only in the Christian doctrine of the fall and the redemption, there was no evidence, even of theism itself, which could really satisfy the mind. It was just here, and perhaps here only, that Pascal's philosophy of religion carried him beyond the atmosphere of his own time and anticipated a position which was to become dominant in the thought of the future.

It is a profoundly important distinction between the philosophy of the seventeenth century and that of to-day that, while the former was content, taking the idea of God from the religious tradition of the civilization out of which it sprang, to employ it in scientific and philosophical speculation as though it were intelligible quite apart from any specifically religious experience, the latter recognizes that the conception of the Absolute to which our general reflection on the world, as known apart from religious experience, may conduct us cannot be as a matter of course interpreted by the religious associations of the word *God*; but that the notion of *God* is, strictly speaking, one only reached through that specific experience which we call religious; so that only as an inference from our acceptance of this as a genuine experience of reality are we at liberty to use that notion in explicating the nature of the Absolute of philosophy. This difference between the part played by the conception of God in the philosophy of the seventeenth century and that played by it in the philosophy of to-day is very largely due to Kant's epoch-making criticism of the old proofs of God's existence and to his association of religion with our moral rather than our scientific experience; but we must acknowledge that Pascal had already reached the latter point of view, although less by means of philosophical criticism than by means of a religious experience which rather diverted him from philosophy altogether than assisted him to reach a position philosophically satisfactory.

But while we must recognize that, as one would
expect, the influence of Descartes is manifest in the
thought of Pascal, there was a thinker of his own
nation, mentioned by himself to M. de Saci along
with Epictetus as one of the authors from whom
he had learned most (as we have already noted),
whose direct effect upon him was vastly greater
than that of Descartes, and is reflected in almost
every page of his writings on the philosophy of
religion. This was Montaigne. And Montaigne
was not of course in the technical sense a 'philosopher'—he was still less so than Pascal's other
favourite thinker, Epictetus ; he is rather the great
representative in literature of a certain attitude towards life, which had always an enormous fascina-
tion for Pascal, while yet it came into violent conflict
with the religious seriousness that was always characteristic of him, and became increasingly so in
the later years of his brief life. What we may call
Montaigne's realism, his clear vision of human life
in all its aspects, including those which men of
another temper are always apt to ignore or to cover
with a veil as disconcertingly ignoble—as well no
doubt as his admirable style—profoundly impressed
one who, like Pascal, desired to 'see life steadily and
see it whole', and who also, as he was in the judgement of his countrymen himself the creator of
modern French prose, had, consciously or no, the
sympathy of a brother craftsman for a master in
the same art. Pascal's own studies in a very different

field—that of mathematical and natural science—
had left him little time or inclination for that wide
ranging over books which made up so much of the
old humanist's business and pleasure; and he was
content for the most part here to live upon the rich
stores which Montaigne's reading had accumulated.
It is indeed rarely that any literary or historical
illustration in Pascal cannot be traced to Montaigne
as its source. But the easy acquiescence of Montaigne in the variegated scene of good and evil which
met his penetrating view,—alike in the world of
human life in general, and in that peculiarly interesting
object of contemplation, his own self, in particular,—
was something from which Pascal was withheld by
the intense moral earnestness by which his character was so remarkably distinguished from that of
his favourite author. The problem of uniting in one
view the frank veracity which was so attractive in
Montaigne with loyalty to a singularly keen perception of the obligation which susceptibility to the
appeal of moral excellence lays upon the conscience
—this problem continually haunted Pascal, and in
the fragments called the *Pensées* we have his attempt
to find its solution in acceptance of what he took to
be the Christian view of humanity's origin, history,
and destiny, unveiled in the Scriptures as interpreted
by the Catholic Church.

We come back then to this—that Pascal was not
what is generally meant by a philosopher at all. It
was with Descartes' science and Descartes' accep-

tance of the obligations of religion that he was in
sympathy; his philosophy rather repelled him.
Montaigne was attractive to him just because he
was not in a technical sense a 'philosopher' at all; for
he offered no system, and attempted no vindication
of religion on grounds of reason accessible to all men.
But he put before his readers with a singular depth
of insight and wealth of illustration the spectacle of
human life without religion; and this was just what
Pascal wanted, if he was to estimate the value of
religion to human life; and to make this estimate,
rather than to understand for the sake of understanding the nature of that which gives unity to all
our various experiences, was Pascal's aim.

Thus the late M. Boutroux was, I think, on the
whole, right in saying that 'in Pascal there was a man
of science (*un savant*), a Christian, and a man'. 'What
he will have nothing to do with is philosophy, that
monstrous association between an object which is
above nature and powers of knowledge which have
no application beyond nature.' [1]

III

PASCAL AND KANT

IN reading these words about Pascal, however,
there may arise in the minds of students of philosophy a recollection which may make them pause
before they refuse to Pascal the title of philosopher

[1] Boutroux, *Pascal*, p. 193.

on the grounds stated by Boutroux. It is the re-collection of Kant, to whom it would certainly be paradoxical to refuse that title. Did not Kant, it may be asked, also propose in his *Critique of Pure Reason* to clear away *knowledge* of the supernatural —of God, Freedom, and Immortality—in order to leave room for *faith*? Did he not do this by showing that our capacities for knowledge were limited to the phenomenal world, so that when we attempt to extend to regions beyond our ordinary experience in space and time the principles which we assume in our inquiries about spatial and temporal pheno-mena, we find ourselves betrayed into illusory and chimerical fancies, which cannot be dignified, as by some philosophers they have been, by the name of knowledge; so that we must fall back on our moral experience as the only trustworthy source, not indeed of *knowledge*, but of a practically effective *faith* in that which our moral experience presupposes, though we are never able to verify its existence by the methods, observation, and inference which we em-ploy in the sciences?

I think that Pascal's position is sufficiently akin to Kant's to make it reasonable to ask whether in re-fusing to him the name of philosopher we do not refuse it to Kant also. But I think that a considera-tion of three points, to which I will proceed to call attention, will show us how far Kant is involved in the condemnation of Pascal (if we are to call it a condemnation of him and not rather the paying

him a compliment) as no philosopher in the proper
sense of the term; and in what ways he is to be
differentiated from Pascal in this respect.

1. It has been said that no one can really claim to
be a philosopher who has not undergone a 'bath of
Spinoza': that is, who has not at any rate felt something of that intellectual passion for unity which
drove Spinoza into his doctrine of a single Substance,
with its consequences in the abandonment of any
God who can reciprocate our love, or any self that
can claim a measure of genuine independence in the
face of a universe wherein every thought and every
movement is completely determined by its place in
the whole all-embracing system which we may call
indifferently Nature or God. A man may have
passed through his 'bath of Spinoza' and ended in
a position in which he can affirm personality in God
and freedom in man in a sense in which Spinoza
would deny them; but his affirmation is not what it
would have been, had he never seriously felt at all
the sting of the thought which inspires what is commonly, in speaking of Spinoza, called his *pantheism*,
and which animates to-day much recent idealism,
both in this country and in Italy. Of Pascal, however, of whom Sainte-Beuve, in the celebrated study
of him which occupies the third book of his work
on Port-Royal, has observed that his was *l'esprit
le moins panthéistique qu'on puisse concevoir*, 'the least
pantheistic mind that it is possible to conceive',[1]

---

[1] *Port-Royal*, t. iii, p. 41 *n.*

we may reasonably doubt whether he had felt this sting or faced this problem. It is indeed his antipathy to lines of thought tending in the direction of Spinoza which divides him so decisively from his elder contemporary Descartes and his junior contemporary Malebranche, whose names are, along with his own, the most distinguished in the roll of the French thinkers of the seventeenth century. Now among those whom all would reckon as in the first rank of philosophers Kant is probably the one whose mind was, in Sainte-Beuve's phrase, *le moins panthéistique*; although the fragments left unpublished after his death, which under the title of *Opus Postumum* have lately been made available for study, show that in the last years of his life he had come to a fuller appreciation of Spinoza's doctrine, which a younger generation of his countrymen than his own had rescued from the obloquy and neglect to which it had long been abandoned.[1] But it is probable that many philosophical critics of Kant would admit that Kant's philosophy suffered through his failure to appreciate the importance of Spinoza; and most of his philosophical critics would agree that the tendency to identify *knowledge* with the kind of apprehension which we have in the mathematical and physical sciences, to the disparagement of any apprehension of objects which are not amenable to the methods of those sciences, is a defect in his system. My first

[1] Cp. on Kant's attitude to Spinoza, my *Kant's Philosophy of Religion*, pp. 82 ff., 179 f.

point is then that Kant did share some of what may be regarded as Pascal's disqualifications for the title of philosopher; and that they are rightly considered as defects in him, even though they may be what the proverb calls *les défauts de ses qualités*, defects closely associated with his merits.

2. But on the other hand there is a great distinction between Kant and Pascal in the fact that Kant's removal of knowledge of the supernatural to make room for faith in it is the issue of a minute and painstaking criticism of our whole cognitive faculty, while Pascal is content with the pregnant remark that *Le cœur a ses raisons que la raison ne connaît pas*. It is, of course, true that Pascal's life ended at an age at which Kant had not yet entered on his so-called 'critical' period; but there is no reason to think that it would ever have occurred to Pascal, or that, even had it occurred to him, he would have regarded it as worth his while or felt it congruous with his genius to conduct an inquiry of this kind.

3. Moreover, there is another distinction between Pascal and Kant which it is relevant to mention in the present connexion, though we must return to it later on. Both may be said to have placed our knowledge of God on a moral rather than on a metaphysical basis; but, while Kant went on to explore the contents and describe the nature of his moral consciousness with, so far as he could achieve it, complete freedom from prepossessions arising from considerations extraneous to that consciousness it-

self, Pascal flung himself on to a revealed system of doctrine and was ready even to flout his moral consciousness where there seemed to be a discrepancy between the two. Here too, it is, I think, clear why we cannot claim for Pascal that he was a philosopher in the sense in which Kant was one, notwithstanding the affinity between their eventual conclusions as to the relation of what we call our scientific knowledge to our apprehension of realities with which the sciences are incompetent to deal.

IV

PASCAL AS EVANGELICAL

IT was indeed far from being the wish of Pascal to be considered a 'philosopher' in respect of his theology. In the famous piece of writing found in Pascal's clothes after his death, and recording his 'definitive conversion' on 23 November 1654, he exclaims: *Dieu d'Abraham, Dieu d'Isaac, Dieu de Jacob, non des philosophes et des savans.*[1] If (with some writers, and especially with Professor Heiler in his great work on Prayer) we classify ideas of God as 'prophetic' or 'philosophical', Pascal's will unquestionably fall into the former group. It will therefore be here in place to dwell for a little upon this contrast between the *prophetic* and the *philosophical* concep-

[1] p. 142.

tions of God, as it will assist us in a comprehension
of Pascal's position. They respectively express two
distinct types of religious experience. By the *prophetic* type of religious experience I mean one the
characteristic of which is a sense of being in the
presence of One higher than ourselves, with whom
we are in a relation only to be described in terms
borrowed from the language appropriate to the
mutual relations of human beings in society. God
speaks to us, commanding, threatening, teaching,
calling, comforting; we speak to him in exclamations
of awe and reverence, in prayer, in submission, in
praise and thanksgiving, in worship and adoration.
Vast as may be the interval between the emotion of
overwhelming terror before what Professor Otto
would call the 'numinous', 'quite other' than ourselves, in whose presence we, like Job, 'abhor
ourselves and repent in dust and ashes',[1] and the
intercourse to which the New Testament invites us,
as of a son with a father, on whose love he can count
as ready to receive and pardon him, however far he
may have gone astray, however grievously he may
have sinned against him; yet both these experiences
and many which bridge the gulf between them have
in common this essential feature—the consciousness
of a personal relation between ourselves and the
Higher than ourselves in whose presence we stand.
This consciousness characterizes pre-eminently the
religious experience of those whom we call *prophets*,

[1] Job xlii. 6.

who come forth from it charged, as it were, with a message to men, whether it be a threatening doom or a gospel of grace, and who, in virtue thereof, gather about them disciples and found religions and churches. But it characterizes also the religious experience of thousands who, though conscious of no such divine commission to their fellows, yet find for themselves the satisfaction of their spiritual aspirations in the realization of a personal intercourse with God through the mediation of his prophets and after the model of that whereof the prophets themselves were conscious and whereof they spake to their disciples. Pascal was not himself the recipient of a prophetic mission; but he was profoundly sensible of being at his conversion admitted through the mediation of Jesus Christ to fellowship with One of whose converse with the men who, beginning with Abraham, Isaac, and Jacob, were chosen to prepare the way of that supreme Prophet the Bible was the record. His idea of God was derived from a religious experience of what I have called the *prophetic* type, which is also the type predominantly, if not exclusively, represented in the Bible.

Yet this is not the only idea of God, nor is the religious experience expressed by it the only type of religious experience which exists. There is also one, the root whereof is a spiritual passion for *unity*, which leads those whom it inspires to dissatisfaction, so long and so far as a gulf is found to divide the soul of the aspirant from anything which presents itself as *real*.

This passion for unity is the driving force in Philosophy, and it may issue in the philosopher in what I should unhesitatingly call a genuine experience of God, as in Aristotle's contemplation of the Unmoved First Mover, whose supreme excellence draws the universe toward himself as the beauty of the beloved draws the lover;[1] or in Spinoza's *amor intellectualis Dei*[2]—the love, consisting in understanding, of that perfect and all-comprehending system which he calls indifferently Nature or God. In such men as these the philosopher's religious experience and his conception of its object seem to be as far as possible removed from those which for convenience I have called *prophetic*.

One sees this especially in the fact that Aristotle and Spinoza—different as are in some important respects their conceptions of the Divine Being, Aristotle making him utterly transcendent, Spinoza wholly immanent—agree in excluding from their theology on principle any recognition of such *reciprocal* intercourse between God and man as that the belief in which constitutes the very stuff of *prophetic* religion. And it was no doubt a keen sense of this kind of difference between the ideas of God, characteristic of the two types of religion respectively, that occasioned Pascal's emphasis upon the difference between the 'God of philosophers and men of science' and the historically revealed personal 'God of Abraham, Isaac, and Jacob' in whom at his 'defini-

[1] See *Metaph. Λ.* 7.   [2] *Eth.* v. 33 ff.

tive conversion' he felt that his soul had found rest at last.

This emphasis might at first sight suggest a doubt whether that intellectual quest of an all-embracing unity which we call philosophy, though capable of association with genuine religious emotion in certain exceptional minds (such as those of Aristotle and Spinoza, to whom I have just referred), is not in itself quite distinct from and alien to the thirst after a living God, in whose presence the worshipper longs to appear, and by whose personal manifestation to himself he believes that all the yearnings of his soul will be satisfied. And this doubt may seem to receive confirmation from the consideration of the undoubted fact that some have succeeded in attaining, by way of a metaphysical criticism of experience, which either ignores or explains as due to illusion the specifically religious consciousness of worshipping communion with a Higher than we, to a view which satisfies their intellectual demand for a vision of reality as an all-embracing unity, but which does *not* arouse in those who hold it that unquestionably religious emotion which inspires certain famous passages of Aristotle's *Metaphysics* and Spinoza's *Ethics*.

Yet, when we remember the phenomenon of *mysticism*, it is impossible to acquiesce in this suggestion of an essential contradiction between the idea of God based on the passion for unity and that based on the thirst after a living God in whose presence we would appear, so that the former can be dismissed as not properly *religious* at all.

Mysticism is a word which has been and is used in many senses. But I think it may be affirmed, with little fear of contradiction, that in the case of those to whom the name of *mystic* would be most generally and with least hesitation applied, the most characteristic feature is a passionate aspiration after unity with the Ultimate Reality—however that be conceived—and the consciousness of at least an incipient or partial realization of such unity. It is obvious that in this characteristic the mystic is akin to the philosopher; his religion, like the other's speculation, is motived by the same passion for unity. But his goal is less an intellectual vision of the unity of all Reality than a consciousness of his own unity with that which is most real.

Now, although it is true that the religious man whose religious experience is of the type which I have called *prophetic* is apt to find the religion of the mystic disconcerting, it would be paradoxical to deny that mysticism is a form of religious experience; it is often indeed regarded (though in my own opinion mistakenly regarded) as religious experience *par excellence*.

In the admirable work of the late Baron von Hügel on *The Mystical Element in Religion* the name of *mystical* is given to an essential factor, one of three essential factors (the others being the *institutional* and the *speculative*), in all religious experience. If this be done, however, it will be necessary to make the term cover aspects of religion which, while they share with mysticism its inward intensity, are *not* characterized by that passionate quest of a consciousness of unity with the all-including Reality which may, I think, be regarded as the hall-mark of mysticism properly so called. It would have in particular to be extended to what I may for the moment call the *evangelical* type of religious experience, a type which is by no means restricted to, but perhaps most easily illustrated from, the records of Protestant piety—by such names, for example, as, to take our own countrymen only, are those of Bunyan, Wesley, Cowper, Catherine Booth. But this kind of religious experience, which issues in an idea of God rather *prophetic* than *philosophical*, is by this very circumstance differentiated from *mysticism* properly so called, since mysticism leads to an idea of God far more akin to the philosophical, inasmuch as it is primarily not so much that of supreme ethical personality as that of the ultimate all-embracing unity.

The piety of Pascal, although this is not always recognized, was rather of this 'evangelical' type than of the 'mystical' type proper. Of no genuine mystic could it be said with any show of plausibility, as we have seen it said of Pascal by Sainte-Beuve, that his mind was 'the least pantheistic that it is possible to conceive'. He was indeed no Protestant, and, despite the fact that he was so deeply and sincerely engaged in a controversy with the Jesuits, who were in possession of the ear of the supreme authority of the Roman Catholic Church, in a matter on which his views and those of his friends approximated in important respects to those of the Reformers, he nowhere shows any sympathy with Protestantism. Indeed, the elaborately ecclesiastical dating of the famous writing found on him after death, containing the record of his conversion on 23 November 1654, 'the day of St. Clement, Pope and Martyr, and others in the martyrology, the eve of St. Chrysogonus and others', well symbolizes his profound consciousness, even in the deepest experiences of his inner religious life, of dependence upon the tradition of the Catholic Church. But his piety was nevertheless of a type which, though perhaps more readily illustrated by Protestant examples, is no more exclusively Protestant than mysticism is exclusively Roman Catholic, despite the attempt of some theologians of the Ritschlian School to identify it with the religious temper of Roman Catholicism.

It is characteristic of what I have called the prophetic type of religious experience as compared with the mystical type that for it *conduct*, rather than contemplation, is central. Pascal illustrates this general rule; but, as I have already mentioned in another connexion, this does not mean that the moral consciousness is made by Pascal the supreme factor in religion, as it is by Kant, and also, I may observe, upon the whole, as I have tried to show elsewhere,[1] by the English Tractarians. I am inclined to think that one

[1] See my *Religious Thought in the Oxford Movement*, pp. 44 ff.

of these, the late Dean Church, in his lecture on Pascal, somewhat exaggerates the place given to the moral consciousness in Pascal's philosophy of religion. No doubt the moral indignation which the casuistry of the Jesuits excited in him and the attraction exercised upon him by the austere standards of Port-Royal sufficiently attest his personal zeal for righteousness. But the lack of confidence in his moral intuitions which is expressed in his readiness to deny their validity in respect of divine action and the place which the celebrated 'wager' takes in his argument on behalf of religion distinguish him, not, in my judgement, to his advantage, from Kant in respect of the rights of what the latter called the 'practical reason' as an organ of religious experience.

Of the 'wager' I will speak later, but of what I have called his lack of confidence in his moral intuitions we have examples in such 'Thoughts' as the following:

'I have passed a great part of my life in the opinion that there is such a thing as justice, and in this opinion I was not mistaken; for God has been pleased to reveal to us that there is. But I did not thus take it; and that was where I was mistaken. I thought that *our* justice was really justice and that I had the means of recognizing Justice and forming a judgement of it.'[1]

Of course such scepticism as this—which, as Sainte-Beuve points out,[2] was too much for such Jansenist

[1] *Pensées*, § 375, p. 500.   [2] *Port-Royal*, iii, pp. 302 ff.

sympathizers as Arnauld and Nicole—knocks the
bottom out of ethics altogether. It is something
quite different from the reflection to be found both
in Plato and in Butler, that where we do not see the
whole of a plan we cannot adequately judge of a
part of it. It is, I think, a proof of Pascal's deficiency
as a philosopher that he does not seem to have
observed this. Again: 'Good God, what stupid talk
is this! *Would God have made the world in order to
damn it? Would he ask so much of beings so feeble?*
and so forth.'[1] Without denying that the stern
doctrines of a now almost obsolete theology were
often the expression not of mere gloomy savagery,
as is sometimes thought, but of a deep sense of sin
and an intense realization of the facts of life; yet one
is shocked by Pascal's inability to allow even a prima
facie difficulty in the contrast between the picture of
God which they suggest and that of the loving
Father revealed in the New Testament. Or lastly:
'What is more contrary to the rules of our miserable
justice than to damn eternally a child incapable of willing
for a sin in which he appears to have so little share? and
yet the nature of man is more difficult to be understood
apart from this mystery than the mystery is difficult for
man to understand.'[2]

Here it is the *tone*—the contempt for those very
intuitions by which we see the superiority of the
greater humanity which distinguishes the social and
legislative ideals of to-day from those of antiquity—

[1] P. § 390, p. 506.   [2] P. § 434, p. 532.

which shocks us. Kant's decisive rejection of the saying *Sunt superis sua jura* as deadly to religion[1] strikes a note here which lifts us to a clearer region than that in which those passages of Pascal show him to have been lingering. There were heights and depths in Pascal which Voltaire was not capable of appreciating; but I think we may recognize here, as well as in the unrelieved pictures of the misery of human life which Voltaire had actually in view, the very large measure of truth in the latter's exclamation: 'Hélas! Pascal, on voit bien que vous êtes malade.'[2] There is undoubtedly something pathological and morbid in the whole outlook of the *Pensées* which one cannot disconnect from their author's bad health—from the deep-seated disease which left him little freedom from pain and ended his life at the early age of thirty-nine.

On the other hand there was a point as to which Pascal unquestionably saw further than Kant; and that is in respect of what Pascal calls the *automate*, 'the psychical mechanism' as we might put it. Although it is possible—through overlooking the importance of the distinction which he draws between the theoretical and the practical Reason—to exaggerate the 'intellectualism' of Kant's ethics, yet I think it is true that he is carried too far by his revulsion from any theory which, like so many that were in vogue

[1] *Ueber das Misslingen aller philosophischen Versuche in der Theodicee, Werke*, ed. Hartenstein, vi, p. 80.
[2] '*Remarques sur les Pensées*' II, *Œuvres*, t. 31, p. 27.

in his day, resolved the claim of the moral law upon us either into the calculated superiority of the pleasures offered by virtue to those to be looked for from vice or into the unmistakable though inexplicable appeal to our taste of certain modes of behaviour. His aversion to all such views led him to a quite unnecessary and unjustified separation of thought from feeling; so that he sometimes gives the impression that he holds virtue to be even incompatible with liking for the virtuous act, an impression which, when brought to book for it by his admirer the poet Schiller, he attempted to remove,[1] but one which his language could not fail, and does not fail, to produce.

Along with this separation of reason from feeling in Kant goes a comparative neglect of the part played in our moral life by what is subconscious and habitual. In strong contrast to this is Pascal's insistence upon the importance of this element. 'Nous sommes automate', he says, 'autant qu'esprit . . . Il faut vivre nos deux pièces, l'esprit par les raisons . . . et l'automate par la coutume . . . *Inclina cor meum, Deus.*'[2] He is much alive—like his countryman and contemporary La Rochefoucauld, who says: 'L'esprit est toujours la dupe du cœur'[3]—to the fact, of which the psychology of to-day makes so much, that the explanation of our actions is often to be found else-

---

[1] '*Religion innerhalb der Grenzen der blossen Vernunft*' I, *Werke*, ed. Hartenstein, vi. p. 117 *n.*

[2] *P.* § 252, p. 449.

[3] *Réflexions morales*, § 102; cp. § 43.

where than in the grounds which we quite sincerely assign in explanation—that our thinking of these indeed is rather itself to be explained by antecedent feelings, which prompt us to the acts that seem to require accounting for thus. Thus Pascal quotes his friend the Duc de Roannez as saying: 'Reasons come to me afterwards, but at first the thing pleases me or shocks me without my knowing the reason of it; and yet it shocks me for the reason which I only discover afterwards.' 'But', says Pascal, 'I do not think that it shocked you for the reasons which are discovered afterwards; rather the reasons are only discovered because the thing shocks.'[1]

This subconscious and habitual factor in mental life, which Pascal sometimes calls *l'automate*, he often, more often, designates by the term *le cœur*, 'the heart'. For example, as we have just seen, the passage in which he insists upon the need of bringing the influence of religion to bear both upon the conscious and rational and upon the subconscious or habitual factors in our constitution ends with the Psalmist's prayer: 'Incline my *heart* unto thy testimonies.' *Le cœur* is here identified expressly with *l'automate*. Let us gather together here some of Pascal's principal statements about *the heart* and see precisely what he means by it. It is contrasted with reason in one of the most celebrated of all his aphorisms: 'Le cœur a ses raisons que la raison ne connaît pas.'[2] The context here shows that he is think-

_____
[1] P. § 276, pp. 457, 458.   [2] P. § 277, p. 458.

ing of the ultimate determination of our conduct
(even where we 'rationalize' it to ourselves or others
by giving reasons for it which are rather invented to
justify it afterwards than its veritable grounds) *not* by
'reasons' such as could form part of a mathematical or
scientific train of argument, but by the relative attraction exercised upon us by one or the other of the two
objects which we have, according to Pascal, a natural
propensity to love—God and ourselves. The love of
God is no more something which we come at by a
process of reasoning than is self-love. 'C'est le cœur
qui sent Dieu et non la raison.'[1] Faith Pascal defines
as *Dieu sensible au cœur, non à la raison.* 'La raison' is
here, as is usual with Pascal, what Kant distinguished
from the *practical* as the *theoretical* Reason—the
Reason employed in the sciences, for which questions
of value have no meaning. The tendency was strong
in the age of Pascal, nor is it extinct to-day—notwithstanding all the criticisms levelled against it by
great thinkers such as Pascal himself and, above all,
by Kant—to demand that Religion should justify
itself on grounds which should take no account of
specific religious experience, but should be such as
might convince men by reasoning from the premises
used in the mathematical and physical sciences or in
that general logic which Aristotle called 'dialectic'.
And in Pascal's age this tendency was reinforced
both by the scholastic tradition, still authoritatively
maintained in the Roman Catholic Church, which

[1] P. § 278, p. 458.

follows St. Thomas Aquinas in claiming that the existence of God can be proved by arguments which take no account of religious experience, and also by the natural inclination of men in an age characterized by a great and sudden advance in mathematical and physical knowledge to look for a triumphant extension of the conquests of the method used in the physical sciences to the whole range of human experience. This inclination had, in Pascal's own country, given birth to what Professor de Burgh[1] has called 'Descartes' splendid vision of a universal mathematics that should unlock all the doors of knowledge'—a vision, by the way, which must be borne in mind in reading Pascal's *L'esprit géométrique*, where it appears as the ideal of scientific method, which it is yet beyond our powers to realize except in the restricted sphere of geometry.

To 'la raison' then is opposed by Pascal 'le cœur'; but 'le cœur a ses raisons', although the context shows, as I have already said, that Pascal's thought in this saying was that our action is often determined, not by grounds which we could, or even by the grounds which we *do* explicitly assign, but by a fundamental attraction to, or love of, either God or self as the case may be, which may not be actually present to our conscious mind at the moment. But, though that be the original significance of the phrase,

[1] In an interesting article on 'Logic and Faith' (well worth reading in this connexion), contributed to the *Journal of Philosophical Studies* for Oct. 1926.

it may be taken as an implicit recognition of the rationality of an intuitive apprehension which can dispense with reasoning. A short note[1] runs as follows: 'Cœur, instinct, principes.'[2] It will serve us as the text for an attempt to draw together the statements of Pascal about 'the heart' and to estimate their value.

It is plain that for Pascal whatever in our mental or spiritual life is other than the pursuit of truth by the method of science is compendiously subsumed under this expression 'le cœur'. *Le cœur* is identified, or at least ranged, with *instinct*, where by 'instinct' one naturally understands that by which we explain the movements of 'l'automate' as we explain our deliberate and reflective acts by 'reason'; it is the word we use for the cause of behaviour in the lower animals which appears to correspond with that which in ourselves is conditioned by conscious design or purpose, whereas in them we seem to find nothing to suggest anything of the kind. Yet in the same phrase *cœur* is also identified or ranged with *principes*. And here we must interpret Pascal's meaning by a reference to a very remarkable 'thought' which runs as follows:[3] 'We know the truth not only by the reason (*la raison*) but also by the heart (*le cœur*); it is in this latter way', i.e. by the heart, 'that we know *first principles*, and it is in vain that

[1] Printed in Brunschvicg's edition in close proximity with the 'thought' we have just been commenting upon.
[2] P. § 281, p. 459.   [3] P. § 282, p. 459.

reasoning, which has no part in them, attempts to contest these. The sceptics, who have this as their sole object, do but waste their pains. We know that we are awake; however we may be unable to prove this by reason, this inability of ours only shows the weakness of our reason, not (as the sceptics assert) the uncertainty of all our knowledge. For the knowledge of first principles, such as the existence of Space, Time, Motion, Number, is as secure as any knowledge obtained by reasoning. And it is on such knowledge, acquired by the heart and by instinct, that reason relies, and takes it for the foundation of all its indirect inferences.'[1] 'The heart', Pascal continues, 'perceives that there are three dimensions in space and that the numerical series is infinite; and reason proves afterwards that there are no square numbers whereof one is double of the other. Principles are directly perceived, propositions are reached as the conclusions of an argument; both with certitude, but by different processes. And it is as useless and as ridiculous for *reason* to demand that *the heart* shall prove its first principles before it will accept them as for *the heart* to demand of *reason* a direct perception of all the propositions that it discovers before it will admit them.' In other words, *le cœur* is here identified with what Aristotle called ὁ νοῦς,

---

[1] This seems to be here the meaning of *discursus*, viz. *indirect* or *mediate inference* as opposed to such direct vision of all that is real *uno intuitu*, in one glance, as we naturally attribute to higher intelligences and to God.

the intuitive apprehension of those first principles of reasoning which reasoning must assume to start with, and which, although in this way distinguished from the discursive, indirect processes which we call *reasoning*, is one with Reason in the highest sense of that word. Such intuitive apprehension of first principles is not rightly, I think, identified with instinct; but in contrast with reasoning they have in common what we may call *immediacy*, and there is thus a recurrent temptation to identify them with one another. Nevertheless we ought, I think, to distinguish those cases in which, as with logical and mathematical principles, we so clearly perceive their truth that we cannot conceive how any proof could make them any more intelligible, and hence feel no need of any such, and those in which we feel on the contrary that our conviction of their truth ('I *feel* quite sure that this is so, but I cannot tell you why') would be, if not more confident, yet more assured of permanence and more communicable to others, if we *could* 'give a reason' for it. Pascal, however, ignores this important distinction and groups *instinctive belief* and *intuitive knowledge* under one head as objects of apprehension by *le cœur*. Lastly, in the thoughts on the difference between *l'esprit de géométrie* and *l'esprit de finesse*,[1] we find the mathematical way of thinking, the process of which he describes at some length in the fragment called *De l'esprit géométrique*,

[1] *P.* § 1. p. 316; cp. also *Discours sur la passion de l'amour*, p. 125.

contrasted with an *esprit de finesse* which is there presented as the 'judgement' which we bring to bear on moral questions (in the widest sense of the word), and which, though not there expressly and in so many words associated with *le cœur*, is certainly regarded as belonging rather to that side of our nature than to *la raison*.

The '*Pensées*' are of course only a collection of unarranged notes, so that one cannot assume that Pascal would not, had he completed them, have done more to unify his terminology than he actually did. Still it is confusing that he should in the same 'thought' use 'esprit' now as the common designation of *l'esprit de géométrie* and *l'esprit de finesse*, now as the name of the former in contrast with *le jugement*, taken as equivalent to the latter. The treatment of the latter is, I may here observe in passing, remarkably akin to the account of 'assent' given in Newman's book *The Grammar of Assent*, which yet does not appear to be indebted to Pascal. The two men have in common a profound interest in those processes of the mind which, while leading to conviction, are carried on below the level of deliberate ratiocination. Both have a genius for describing their deepest personal experiences, the one in striking and memorable phrases, the other in periods of haunting beauty. Neither is a systematic thinker, and our admiration of the delicacy of their perceptions and the aptness of their language cannot conceal from us their failure to recognize that necessity for a rigorous examination of the meaning of each word used (I am not of course thinking of Pascal's mathematical and scientific writings) and of consistency in usage which is expected of a philosopher in the strict sense of the term. No doubt few philosophers, if any, are free from all reproach in this matter; but Pascal seems hardly to have felt any obligation to aim at such accuracy of statement.

We find then, I think, a profounder consciousness in Pascal than in Kant of what we may call the history (or, if we like, the psychology) of our moral consciousness, but a far less clear grasp of its essential nature as a consciousness of *unconditional* obligation, such as can only be laid upon us by a law intuitively recognized as good in itself, not merely as commanded by a superior or as conducive to our happiness.

We have seen how this defect in Pascal's view led to his readiness to flout his moral intuitions when they conflicted with what tradition led him to regard as revealed truth; thus abandoning in principle that critical office of the moral consciousness, which is the most important agent of the historical development of religion. We have now to see how it led to a surprising lapse from the 'disinterestedness' which, as Kant so powerfully showed, is an essential feature of morality, into what appears, at first sight at any rate, to be in principle a sheer eudaemonism or utilitarianism, strangely out of keeping with the austere and self-sacrificing piety of Pascal himself.

Now students of the history of ethical thought will here recall that a similar charge has often been made against Kant on the ground of his so-called 'moral argument for the existence of God' from the necessity of supposing a Being in whom goodness of will is conjoined with sovereign power over nature, in order to award to virtue the happiness which it deserves, but which in this world it so often fails to obtain. Perhaps I may be allowed to quote here what I have said elsewhere[1] upon this subject:

'What, it may be asked, has become of the boasted disinterestedness of Kant's ethics, whereby they are supposed to be so remarkably distinguished from all and every form of Eudæmonism, if they be held to postulate a Being willing and able to award Happiness to Virtue and a capacity in ourselves to participate in the engagement of that award?'

We must remember that Kant holds the immortality of the soul to be thus postulated as well as the existence of God.

'On this point, however, I think that Kant has an adequate reply. He never fails to insist that any such award of Happiness to Virtue can never serve as a motive to duty without rendering the volition which is thus motived totally destitute of moral value; but it appears to him unquestionable, that when the conception of a world in which Happiness is awarded to Virtue is presented to the mind—and this "Reason points out" (to quote his own words) "to all rational beings as the goal of all their moral wishes"— it becomes our duty to promote that

[1] *Kant's Philosophy of Religion*, pp. 64, 65.

Highest Good; and, since we cannot be bound to do what is impossible, the possibility of this Highest Good is thus *postulated*. Now this implies for Kant both that Virtue can be perfectly attained (which involves the immortality of the soul) and that there is a Being with the power and will to crown that Virtue with Happiness. Readers of Plato's *Republic* will recall the passages in which it is agreed to inquire whether justice is or is not to our advantage, apart altogether from the expectation of any rewards, whether in this life or in the next; and in which, when at last, but only after Justice has been ascertained to be "the health of the soul", the question of its advantageousness has answered itself, the rewards are restored to it and the ultimate supremacy of the Good in the universe invoked in support of the belief in an immortal life for the soul, wherein the issues of life are worked out according to a just law. I do not think that there can be denied to be a demand made, as it were, by the moral consciousness upon the world, which is quite distinct from a desire for personal happiness, apart from the hopes of attaining which one would not count it worth while to be good; as may be proved by this claim being quite compatible with an acceptance as just by an individual of his own exclusion, as undeserving, from the happiness which he yet demands that those who deserve it shall attain. Thus I do not hold that the Kantian doctrine of the *Summum Bonum* . . . can be fairly described as a relapse from the disinterestedness of his ethical teaching into Eudæmonism.'

We must now inquire whether we can also acquit Pascal of a lapse of this kind in his celebrated doctrine of the wager.

V

PASCAL'S WAGER

To understand this doctrine, it will be well to have in our minds the passage in which Pascal brings it forward.[1] It runs thus:

'If there is a God, he is infinitely incomprehensible; since, having neither parts nor limits, he has no relation to us. We are therefore incapable of knowing what he is, or even that he is. This being so, who will dare to undertake the resolution of this question? Certainly not we, who have no relation to him. Who then can blame Christians for not being able to render a reason for their belief, they who profess a religion for which they cannot render a reason? They declare, when expounding it to the world, that it is a "foolishness"' (he is referring to St. Paul's saying in 1 Cor. i. 21. 'It pleased God by the *foolishness* of preaching to save them that believe')— 'and after that do you complain of their not proving it? If they proved it, they would be inconsistent; in failing to prove it they are found not to fail in knowing their own minds. Yes, but even if this may excuse those who present the Christian religion as unproved, and exempts them from blame on account of bringing it forward without rendering a reason for it, yet it does not excuse those who accept it. Let us now examine this point and say "God either exists or he does not". But to which alternative are we to lean? Reason cannot decide at all. There is an infinite gulf fixed between us and God. There

[1] P. § 233. pp. 436 f.

is a game being played right away at this infinite distance, where there will turn up either heads or tails. Upon which will you bet? You have no rational grounds for choosing either one or the other; you cannot give reasons to defend either choice. Do not therefore blame those who have made a choice; for you know nothing of the probabilities. "No, but I will blame them for having made, not this particular choice, but any choice at all; for though the man that says 'heads' and he that says 'tails' may be equally in fault, they are both in fault; the right thing to do is not to bet at all." Yes, but one *must* bet; this is not optional, you are committed to it. On which side then will you bet? Let us see. Since one has to choose, let us see which is the alternative in which you have less interest. You have two things to risk: truth and well-being; two things to stake: your reason and your will, your know-ledge and your happiness; there are two things which you would naturally avoid: error and misery. Your reason is no way outraged by either choice, since you must necessarily make a choice. You may then dismiss that consideration. But what about your happiness? Let us weigh the profit and loss involved in betting on the existence of God. Let us consider these two alternatives: If you win, you win all; if you lose, you lose nothing. Bet then on his existence without hesitation. "Excellent," you say, "I agree that one must bet: but perhaps I am betting too much." Let us see. Since the risk of winning or losing is equal, if you only stood to win two lives and only lose one, you might still be well advised to make this wager; but if you stood to win three, you ought to make it (since you cannot refuse to play at all), and you would be rash, being compelled to play, not to risk your life to gain three in a game where there is an equal chance of winning or losing. But it is not a question of two or three lives against one; there is an eternity of life and happiness to be won. That being so, were there an infinite number of chances and only one of them in your favour, you would still be right in taking a bet of two to one against your fancy; and you would be unwise, being obliged to play, to refuse to take a bet of three to one against it, where out of an infinite number of chances, there is one for you, supposing that you stood to win in that case an infinity of infinitely happy life. But in this case there is an infinity of infinitely happy life to win; there is one chance of winning, and the chances of losing are limited to a definite number; moreover you only stand to lose something which is itself finite. This removes all equality between the alternatives; where there is an infinity on one side, and where there is not an infinite number of chances of losing to set against the chance of winning, there is no ground for hesitation; the right course is to stake everything. And thus when one is forced to play, one must admit that there is no reason for securing one's life rather than risk it for the infinite gain, the chance of winning which is equal to that of losing what in comparison of infinity is nothing at all.

'For it is of no use to say that it is uncertain whether one will win, and certain that one is running a risk, and that the infinite distance which exists between the certainty of what one is risking and the uncertainty of what one stands to gain, makes the finite good which one is certainly risking equal to the infinite good which is uncertain. It is not so. Every gambler risks what he

certainly has to win what he is uncertain of getting; and
yet, in his certain risk of a finite good for the uncertain
chance of gaining a good which is also finite, he is not
sinning against reason. There is not an infinite distance
between this certainty of what is risked and the uncertainty
of the gain; it is false to suppose that there is. There is
indeed an infinite distance between the certainty of
winning and the certainty of losing. But the uncertainty
of winning is proportionate to the certainty of what one
risks according to the proportion borne by the chances
of winning to those of losing. That is why if there are
as many risks on the one side as on the other, the bet is
even; and in that case the certainty of what is risked is
equal to the uncertainty of the gain; so far is it from being
infinitely distant. And so our proposition is of an infinite
force, when there is what is finite to stake in a game where
the chance of winning and losing are equal, and we stand
to gain what is infinite. This is demonstratively true; and
if there is any truth which men are capable of perceiving,
it is this.'

Now perhaps the first criticism of this celebrated
argument—which it is possible, as the note in Brunschvicg's edition conjectures, was suggested to him
by a passage in Raymond of Sebonde's *Theologia
Naturalis*,[1] which Montaigne's *Apologie* may have
led him to read—is that it is unworthy of the dignity
of the subject. This criticism was actually made by
Voltaire. But on consideration it has little weight.
It must be borne in mind that Pascal was interested

[1] c. 58. Cp. my *Studies in the History of Natural Theology*,
p. 310.

in the odds not as a gambler but as a mathematician who had bestowed no little thought on the calculus of probabilities.

Associated as it was in his mind with those scientific studies his passion for which was only less than his passion for God, it probably never occurred to him to think that a wager was, as such, something not to be named on the same page with God. I know no better commentary on the passage than that to be found in William James's *The Will to Believe*.[1] Not only are the remarks in this essay on Pascal's argument itself well worthy of attention, but James's own argument is in principle the same as that of Pascal, and it is expressed, not (it may be) with the same perfection of style, but in a way which avoids what may easily repel a sensitive reader in Pascal's. For unquestionably, taken in connexion with other 'thoughts',[2] the alternative is on the whole presented by him in a form quite eudaemonistic—as eternal happiness in the one event, eternal misery in the other. By James, on the other hand, notwithstanding his 'pragmatism', the Supreme Good, in which he contends that we are justified in believing, though we cannot prove its reality, because, as he puts it, 'our passional nature not only lawfully may but must decide an option between propositions, whenever it is a genuine option that cannot by its nature

[1] One of the earliest and, in my judgement, one of the best of his writings, which gave its name to a volume of essays, published in 1897, in which it stood first.
[2] e.g. *P.* §§ 194 and 195, pp. 415 ff.

be decided on intellectual grounds; for to say, under such circumstances, "Do not decide" but leave the question open is itself a passional decision—just like deciding yes or no—and is attended with the same risk of losing the truth'—this Supreme Good is not described eudaemonistically, nor is the alternative to losing it depicted in terrific colours, as an endless life of misery with which unbelievers are threatened by God. The real force of Pascal's argument is however, I think, not lost in James's version. It must, however, be confessed that we miss in Pascal that insistence on the disinterestedness of morality, which, as we have seen, is not abandoned by Kant even in his postulation of God and immortality. We have indeed to bear in mind that the argument from the wager (which is said not to be mentioned in the earliest sketch of Pascal's projected Apology for Christianity)[1] is intended rather for libertines, who are supposed inaccessible to considerations of a less selfish nature, than for men who could be won by the congruity of religion with their own best aspirations. One must not think, for a moment, of Pascal himself as believing merely on the ground of this argument. But Pascal cannot be said to have done anything in his presentation of the case for religion to discourage the eudaemonism—crude rather than simple—which characterizes so much of the ethical and religious thought of the seventeenth and eighteenth centuries, and which finds at last its grand

[1] See *Pensées et Opuscules*, ed. Brunschvicg, p. 438 *n*. 1.

critic in Kant, with his account of the moral consciousness as the consciousness of a Categorical Imperative. Kant's philosophy of religion may, indeed, be criticized on the ground that religion has other roots than that in the moral consciousness, whereas Kant tends to regard it as a mere appendix to the latter. But he brings out all the more for that reason the importance of the office of the moral consciousness in the criticism of religious tradition, in discharging which it becomes the principal agent in the progressive development of religion. This is not brought out at all by Pascal, since he is content, as we have seen, to allow the religious tradition to control our acceptance of the deliverances of our moral consciousness.

VI

PASCAL AND THE ARGUMENT FROM DESIGN

IN Kant insistence upon the dependence of religion on the moral consciousness was associated with the criticism and rejection, to the importance of which in the history of modern theology I have already referred, of the non-religious proofs of God's existence, which had played so large a part in the teaching of the schools down to that time. On this matter Pascal would have been with Kant. Though he does not enter like Kant upon a detailed criticism of these arguments, he quite decisively declines to

rest his faith in God on any grounds which ignore
or abstract from a specifically religious experience.
And it is noticeable that whereas Kant's severest
criticism is reserved for the Ontological Argument,
which argues to the reality of God from the presence
of the idea of God in our minds, while the Argument
from Design in nature is always mentioned by him
with respect, although he holds its formal statement
to be logically unsatisfactory—it is with this latter
argument that Pascal exhibits peculiar impatience;
an impatience all the more noticeable in a great in-
vestigator, such as he was, of natural phenomena;
for as a rule men of science, if religious at all, have
delighted to trace the vestiges of a Creator in the
world which they have made it their business to
explore.

We turn to Pascal's strictures on the Argument
from Design in nature.[1]

'I wonder at the boldness with which these men'—he
is speaking, it would seem, of writers on 'natural
theology'—'undertake to speak of God. In addressing
their observations to men destitute of religion, they deal
in their first chapter with the proof of the Divinity from
the works of nature. I should not be surprised at this
undertaking of theirs, did they address themselves to
believers, for there is no question but that they who
possess a lively faith within their hearts see at once that
all which exists is but the work of the God whom they
worship. But for those in whom this light of faith is

---

[1] P. §§ 242–247, pp. 445 ff.

extinct, and in whom one aims at causing it to revive, those lacking faith and grace, who, while seeking with all the light they possess whatever they can find in nature which may lead them to that knowledge, find nothing but obscurity and darkness; to tell *them* that they have only to look at the least of those things which surround them, and they will see God manifested there; and to give them for evidence of this great and important matter only the courses of the moon and the planets, and to pretend that one have thus proved what one promised to prove; this is to give the unbelievers good ground for believing the evidences of our religion to be very weak; and both reason and experience convince one that nothing is more apt to arouse in their minds a feeling of contempt for it. It is not thus that Scripture, which knows better than these writers the things which belong to God, speaks of them. It says that God is a God that hideth himself, and that, after the corruption of man's nature by the fall, he has left men in a state of blindness from which they can only be delivered by Jesus Christ, apart from whom all communication with God is cut off. "No man knoweth the Father save the Son, and he to whom the Son hath willed to reveal him."

'This is what Scripture shows us, when it says in so many passages that they who seek after God find him. One does not speak thus of a light like that of the sun at noon-day. One does not say that those who seek the sun at noon-day, or water in the sea, will find it; and so it is clear that the evidence of God in nature is not of this obvious kind. And so Scripture tells us elsewhere. "Verily thou art a God that hidest thyself." [1]

[1] *P.* § 242, pp. 445, 446.

'It is a remarkable thing that no canonical writer has ever made use of nature to prove the existence of God. All aim at making us believe in him. David, Solomon and the rest did not say "There is no vacuum in nature, therefore there is a God". They must have been cleverer than the cleverest who have come after and have all used this kind of argument. This is very noteworthy.' [1]

One is not surprised to find Voltaire[2] recalling the Psalmist's exclamation[3] 'The heavens declare the glory of God', as contradicting this sweeping statement of Pascal. But Pascal would presumably have said that they declare it only to those who are believers already. He goes on: ' "What? (he imagines an objector saying) Do you not yourself affirm that the heaven and the birds prove God?" No. "And does not Religion say so?" No. For although that be true in a sense, for certain souls on whom God has bestowed this illumination, yet it is false in respect of the greater part of mankind.' [4]

Pascal stands here in the most striking contrast with Kant. The philosopher of Königsberg, as we know from a famous passage in the *Critique of Practical Reason*[5] and from a celebrated incident narrated by an eyewitness,[6] was especially moved by the spectacle of the starry heavens and the

[1] *P.* § 243, pp. 446, 447.
[2] *Remarques*, II, *Œuvres*, t. 31, p. 25.
[3] Ps. xix. 1.
[4] *P.* § 244, p. 447.
[5] *Werke*, ed. Hartenstein, v. 167.
[6] Wasianski, *Kant in seine letzten Lebensjahren*, pp. 192 f.

observation of the wonderful instincts of birds—
just the two things of the testimony of which Pascal
speaks so slightingly—not indeed accounting them
to be logically demonstrative proofs, but certainly
finding in them evidence irresistible to his own
mind of a divine world-ordering Reason.

Yet it was Kant, as we have seen, who, notwithstanding his personal susceptibility to the impression of design which nature makes upon the human
mind, the cultured as well as the unsophisticated,
by his drastic criticism of the attempt to turn that
impression into an argument and of the metaphysical
assumptions which, as he contended, were implied
in the use of that argument, brought to an end the
reign of the old 'natural theology', against which
Pascal, with his refusal to be content with the 'God
of philosophers and men of science', had long before
revolted. For the thinkers of the seventeenth and
eighteenth centuries—with notable exceptions, such
as that of Pascal himself or, to take a very different
and later example, of the poet Blake, who inveighs
against 'natural theology' as an 'impossible absurdity'[1]
were apt to treat theology as the 'last chapter of a
non-religious metaphysic';[2] but for those of our day
it is the science of religious experience; and when
we discuss the nature of the ultimate Unity or of the
supreme Individuality, we do not speak of ourselves
as dealing with the problem of the nature of God,
unless we explicitly take into account—as indeed

[1] *Milton*, p. 42. 13.   [2] *Concepts of Continuity*, p. 240.

I think we are bound at some point to do—the witness of such specifically religious experience.

It is, I think, a curious and interesting fact in the history of religious thought that now, when the general tendency of thought upon this subject is set in the direction in which Pascal, the devoted Roman Catholic, was guided by his religion, the Roman Catholic Church has become, in a changed intellectual world, the special champion of the rights of the old natural theology. The Vatican Council has condemned the view that the existence of God cannot be certainly known by the light of reason from the things that he has made; and the opinion, to which Pascal at any rate sometimes approximates, that there is no genuine knowledge of God except through the Christian revelation, while it has found defenders among Protestant theologians, is recognized as being quite definitely inconsistent with Catholic tradition. Indeed, some of the Ritschlian school in particular have on that very account even accused the Catholic tradition—I do not say justly —of deriving its idea of God rather from Pagan sources—from Plato and Aristotle, Plotinus and Proclus—than from the Gospel of Jesus Christ. There was scarcely any feature of this same tradition, on the other hand, wherein that loyal Roman Catholic and profoundly Christian spirit, the late Friedrich von Hügel, loved more strongly to insist than on its generous recognition and utilization of non-Christian contributions to our knowledge of the

God whose fullest revelation of himself is made in the person and work of the Founder of the Christian religion.

In this respect, however, Pascal's bent is in quite a different direction from that of the traditional Catholic theology. He disparages, as we have seen, the Argument from Design in nature as useless except for men who are already believers. Keenly interested as he was in the investigation of natural phenomena, he seems (as Sainte-Beuve has observed)[1] to have been impressed rather with terror at the infinite realms of space disclosed by science than filled with the rapture which the same revelation inspired in a Giordano Bruno, or, like Newton and Kant and many a 'devout astronomer', moved to awestruck worship by the wisdom displayed in the order of the starry heavens. And if his religion was thus dissociated from the scientific experience which was his in so rich a measure, he was nevertheless always a man of science rather than a humanist; he had little love or veneration for the great tradition of secular philosophy and culture, and shows little sympathy with or understanding of any religious experience, pagan or even Jewish, which is not definitely Christian. His great admiration for Epictetus—than whom, as he told M. de Saci, few had known better man's duty towards God, and whom, he said, one might have even been tempted to worship, had he but known his impotence to perform

[1] *Port-Royal*, iii, p. 39.

that duty—may be alleged as a disproof of this statement. But it is the exception which proves the rule: the only school of classical thought which attracts him is that Stoicism of the Roman Empire whose kinship of tone and temper to that of their contemporaries, the first preachers of Christianity, created the very ancient legend of a friendly correspondence between Seneca and St. Paul.

The pagan's God, says Pascal, is but a geometrical truth; the Jew's but an earthly providence; only the Christian's is his sole Good.[1] He appears to forget that the cry 'Whom have I in Heaven but thee, and there is none upon earth that I desire in comparison of thee',[2] is in the Scriptures which the Jew shares with the Christian; and he oddly enough contrasts with the God of the Jews 'the God of Abraham, the God of Isaac, the God of Jacob, the God of the Christians'. 'We have no knowledge of God', he declares, 'except in Jesus Christ.' Thus he anticipates, as I have already pointed out, not only the recognition, familiar since Kant's criticism of the old natural theology, that the knowledge of God in the sense which the word bears for religion cannot be reached by any argument which abstracts altogether from specifically religious experience, but even the exaggerated 'Christo-centricism' of a theological school which started from Kantian principles, but in this matter at any rate reached conclusions which would have been extremely unacceptable to Kant himself.

[1] P. § 556, p. 581.   [2] Ps. lxxiii. 25.

VII

PASCAL AND THE FALL OF MAN

WE come now to the point which is the pivot upon which Pascal's philosophy of religion turns: the acknowledgement of original sin and the consequent alienation of man from God, in whom alone nevertheless the human spirit, which, in Augustine's famous words, he has made for himself, can find rest and satisfaction;[1] and the necessity, if this alienation is to be overcome, and the human spirit to attain to this the only goal of its desires, of such a Mediator as the Christian Religion proclaims Jesus Christ to be.

The evidence of man's fall Pascal finds in the paradoxical union in man of greatness and littleness, of high aspirations and ideals with impotence to realize them. Upon this subject he expends all his eloquence. Let me quote one of his most remarkable sayings.[2] 'Quelle chimère est-ce donc l'homme? Quelle nouveauté, quel monstre, quel chaos, quel sujet de contradiction, quel prodige! Juge de toutes choses, imbécile ver de terre; dépositaire du vrai, cloaque d'incertitude et d'erreur; gloire et rebut de l'univers.' One cannot but recognize here the original of some famous lines in Pope's *Essay on Man* which must have been directly inspired by this outburst of Pascal's:

[1] See Aug. *Conf.* i. 1.   [2] P. § 434, p. 531.

Placed on this isthmus of a middle state,
A being darkly wise and rudely great;
With too much knowledge for the sceptic side,
With too much weakness for the stoic's pride.

(here the poet is no doubt recalling Pascal's favourite
contrast of Montaigne and Epictetus with their
opposite misrepresentations of human nature.)

He hangs between; in doubt to act or rest,
In doubt to deem himself a god or beast:
In doubt his mind or body to prefer;
Born but to die, and reasoning but to err.
Alike in ignorance his reason such,
Whether he thinks too little or too much;
Chaos of thought and passion, all confused;
Still by himself abused or disabused;
Created half to rise and half to fall,
Great lord of all things, yet a prey to all;
Sole judge of truth, in endless error hurled,
The glory, jest, and riddle of the world.

It is curious to note Voltaire's impatient comments
on Pascal's insistence on the paradoxical enigmatic
character of human nature. He can see no substance
in it.

'Man is not a riddle, as you'—that is, Pascal—'make
him out to be for the pleasure of solving it. Man seems
to be well adapted to his place in the order of nature.
Superior to the animals whom he resembles in his bodily
organs; inferior to other beings whom he probably resembles in his capacity of thinking, he is, like everything
else that we observe, mingled of good and evil, of

pleasure and pain. He is furnished with passions to move him to action and with reason to control his actions. Were he perfect, he would be God; and these supposed contrarieties which you call *contradictions* are but the necessary factors in the composition of man, who is, like everything else in nature, just what he ought to be.' 'I grant', he says, 'that man is in a sense inconceivable; but all the rest of nature is so too; and there are no more contradictions to be found in man than in any other being.' [1]

The important words for our purpose in Voltaire's remarks are those with which they end—that man, like everything else in nature, is *what he ought to be (ce qu'il doit être)*. Now this is precisely what Pascal denies. Let us see how it was possible that two acute observers should take such opposite views of the spectacle of human nature.

Those who are familiar with the *Nicomachean Ethics* of Aristotle will remember the method by which he sets out to arrive at the principles which should determine human conduct. He assumes that everything which exists in nature has some end on its success in realizing which depends its title to be called *good* of its kind. But how are we to tell what in any particular instance this *end* is? Only by considering what the thing *does*, and disentangling that which it alone can do or at least does better than any other kind of thing. In the case of man we find that man *grows*—but no better than a plant; *feels*—but

[1] *Remarques, Œuvres*, t. 22, pp. 30, 31.

no better than a beast; and *thinks*—which no other being known to us can do. Hence in the activity of *thought*, in the widest sense, we find the end of human nature, by the successful performance of which he becomes entitled to be called a *good* man. Now Voltaire is faithful to this ancient Aristotelian method of approaching the valuation of human life. He, after Aristotle, assumes the perfection of nature—like everything else in nature, he says, man is what he ought to be. *Nature does nothing in vain* is the principle of Aristotle. Like Aristotle, at any rate in the programme outlined at the beginning of the *Ethics*, he treats man as just a part of nature like any other—treating him *objectively*, so to say, as we might treat anything else which we only know *from without*, instead of starting from that knowledge of human nature *from within*, which we have as we have it not of the nature of any other being, just because this human nature is *our own*.

It is obvious that this method is one which is least satisfactory where we have such knowledge from within, and only completely satisfactory where we not only do not have such knowledge, but cannot have it, because there is none to have, as in the case of artefacts. We can safely assume that an artefact was made for a certain definite purpose, and if we do not know what this was, we should ascertain it in the way suggested by Aristotle. Thus a clock, though it might serve as a paper-weight or a missile, would plainly so serve no better than many other

things, such as a book or a chair; but only a thing
with the complicated machinery which it has, and
a book or a chair has not, can tell the time; and we
are therefore quite satisfied with regarding this as
the end or purpose for which the clock was made,
and reckoning it as a *good* clock according as it
succeeds in telling the time accurately and depend-
ably. In the case of living things other than man,
the method of valuation does not satisfy us so completely. We cannot with the same conviction state
an end for which they are made; and though we may
not be able to attribute to them themselves a consciousness of any end, we may have to acknowledge
that they have *feelings* of their own, and that these
need not always be pleasant or painful (even if
normally and on the whole they are so) according as
the individual beings are in the way of success or of
failure in the attainment of what *we* may regard as
the end of their specific nature; and, at any rate, a
new criterion, an inward one, is introduced, even
though *we* may not be in a position to do more than
guess at it. But when we come to human beings, we
have not merely to reckon with pleasant and painful
feelings, our own or our fellows', and, if theirs, by
them communicable to us, but with our rational consciousness of an end and of a moral obligation. It
is the imperishable merit of Kant to have pointed
out with greater decision and clearness than any
other thinker the character of our moral consciousness as a consciousness of unconditional obligation,

which is not dependent upon any conclusion otherwise reached as to the nature of the *end* for which we are created, but which rather itself reveals to us that end in the accomplishment of our *duty*, whatever that may be.

Pascal may not, as I have already hinted, have understood so clearly as Kant what the latter called the autonomy of our moral consciousness; but this did not hinder him from approaching the problem of human destiny, not, with Voltaire, from an external point of view, as we might that of a thing with no inner nature of its own or none of which we can take cognizance, but, as Kant did, from the point of view of the moral consciousness. It was from this point of view that it did not appear possible to him as it did to Voltaire to say that man was *ce qu'il doit être*. From Voltaire's point of view man was intelligible enough; since from that point of view one learns what a thing ought to be from what it is; and the distinction between the two reduces itself to that between the specific and the individual nature; as we may speak of a horse as a bad horse, not because it could or, therefore, in any intelligible sense, *ought to* gallop faster than it does, but because it does not gallop so fast as the normal horse can, and therefore as you require it to do, having bought it as a specimen of its kind with a view to your use of the capacities belonging to the normal specimen of that kind. So of a man we may say that he is a bad scholar or a bad cricketer or a bad cook; but we

do not regard these as necessarily adverse judge-
ments on the moral character of the individuals who
fail in those occupations. Now we have here to do
with a dividing line of the utmost importance between different groups of thinkers. It is from the
moral consciousness and the sense of sin which
waits upon it that there arises a perpetually renewed
protest by the most sensitive and some of the most
practically effective spirits against what may be called
the naturalistic view of the world. To regard the
moral consciousness as wholly explained by an immanent urge in individuals of a species to the performance of actions normally conducive to the
interests of the species, and the sense of sin as merely
the result of a discrepancy between the aspirations
which that urge implants and the capacities of the
individual, who, though he may not be what, as a
human being, he *ought* to be, could not be other, as
an individual, than what he is; this is a view which
must ever be attractive and plausible to those who
are content to regard the voice which speaks in them
with, in Butler's phrase, 'manifest authority'[1] as
essentially a deceptive trick played upon them by
nature, and its *feierliche Majestät*, as Kant called it,[2]
its 'solemn air of sovereignty', as in fact an illusion.
Against that we have to set just this consciousness
itself—the sense of sin and the sentiment of remorse
where what is taken to be our duty has been disre-
garded. A naturalistic explanation of the moral con-

[1] *Serm.* II.   [2] *Kr. d. prakt. V.* (ed. Hartenstein, v, p. 82).

sciousness accepted by the understanding may no doubt kill that sense of sin and that sentiment of remorse; but it can very rarely destroy a sense of obligation *somewhere*—perhaps a sense of obligation to be veracious at all costs 'though it were to their own mischief':[1] a sense often particularly strong in men whose scientific theories can allow it no theoretical basis. Thus we have left on our hands a quite unresolved contradiction in our souls between an apparently self-evidencing authority and an intellectual assent to a theory which is inconsistent with that authority. This unresolved contradiction is after all a greater scandal to philosophy than is involved in a frank acknowledgement of the authority of the moral law speaking in our conscience along with a recognition of the mystery which is involved both in the inability of the man to fulfil the obligation thus laid upon him and also in the difficulty of finding in the world satisfactory evidence of a government in accordance with demands suggested by the moral consciousness—such an acknowledgement as we find in Pascal, in Butler, and in Kant.

All these thinkers are agreed that man is *not* what Voltaire says he is, *ce qu'il doit être*, that which he ought to be; and all of them find here the necessity for a doctrine of *original sin*. Pascal and Butler accept the doctrine which they found propounded in the traditional teaching of the Christian Church, Pascal insisting that it alone accounted for his own

[1] Ps. xv. 4.

spiritual experience and that which was reflected in the juxtaposition in the world's philosophical literature of the lofty ideals of an Epictetus with the realism of a Montaigne, while Butler contends that, whatever difficulties may be legitimately found in it, it is 'a thing throughout and particularly analogous to what we see in the daily course of natural Providence'.[1]

Kant sat looser than either Pascal or Butler to the authority of religious tradition; and any reassertion of original sin, of a 'radical evil', as Kant calls it, in human nature, was quite alien from the spirit of the so-called Enlightenment, of which Voltaire was the most conspicuous literary representative and with which Kant's philosophical antecedents led him (in a general way) to sympathize. Nor could he, with Pascal and Butler, accept the biblical legend of Adam's fall as accounting for (though he was at pains to show that it aptly symbolized) the fact which he found writ large on the page of history, and testified to by what every individual soul, when once it has attained to the stage of reflecting upon its own moral experience, discovers to hold good within itself.

This is the fact to which St. Paul has given classical expression in the Epistle to the Romans, 'To will is present with me, but how to perform that which is good I find not; the good that I would I do not, but the evil that I would not, that I do'.[2] That is our

[1] *Analogy*, Ps. 2 c. 5, § 5. [2] Rom. vii. 18, 19.

personal experience; and it is also that of the race to which we belong. 'We have proved both Jews and Gentiles, that they are all under sin—as it is written, There is none righteous, no, not one.'[1] To Kant the *fact* of *original sin* is indubitable, but, like that of the freedom of the human will with which it is clearly associated, it is *inscrutable*. The traditional explanation which treats it as *inherited*—whether after the fashion of a disease, of a legal disability, or of a ceremonial impurity—fails to account for the essential feature of the case that we account *ourselves* responsible for what we do amiss, although we cannot trace our propensity thus to do amiss exclusively to a source within our own individual conscious life.

It is not with Kant's theory of original sin, however, that we are here concerned, but with Pascal's. He, characteristically, with the readiness we have already noted in him to subordinate his reason and even his moral intuitions to the authority of ecclesiastical tradition, is content to explain our condition of inability to fulfil the law, of an obligation to fulfil which we are notwithstanding convinced, by means of the story related in Genesis concerning the first progenitors of mankind. But, as I have throughout found it instructive to compare and contrast Pascal with Kant, I think it important to emphasize their agreement in giving a central place in their philosophy of religion to a doctrine of original sin. Here

[1] Rom. iii. 9, 10.

they are together in the recognition, to which they are compelled by the profundity of their insight into the facts of moral experience, of a mystery therein which Voltaire denies to be more than a mystification; and therefore neither of them acquiesce in Voltaire's assertion that man like the rest of nature is what he ought to be, *ce qu'il doit être*. We may here, perhaps, recall a third witness to the necessity of this recognition from a different quarter: I mean the poet Browning's commendation of Christianity on the ground that it led the way in proclaiming so essential a truth.

> I still to suppose it true for my part
> See reasons and reasons; this, to begin:
> 'Tis the faith that launched point blank her dart
> At the head of a lie—taught Original Sin,
> The Corruption of Man's Heart.[1]

Pascal, finding man thus alienated from the God in whom alone he can find the full satisfaction of his whole nature, is led straight to the need of a Mediator between God and man, and thence to the acknowledgement of Jesus Christ as such a Mediator. Following the plan I have followed so far, I will here again indicate the relation in which his view stands to that of Kant. In principle Kant agrees with Pascal in affirming the necessity of a reconciliation between God, conceived as the giver of the moral law with its inexorable and unconditional demands, and man with his obligation to obey it and his in-

[1] *Gold Hair; A Story of Pornic.*

ability perfectly to fulfil that obligation under the actual conditions in which he finds himself. Thus he also teaches a doctrine of Atonement, whereof he takes that taught by the Church to be a figure or symbol. Kant's doctrine of Atonement may be shortly expressed in some such way as this. There is an ideal of humanity well pleasing to God, by making which the guiding principle of our conduct we do all that we can, in the faith that God takes the change of heart at conversion, when the converted person becomes 'a new man', in discharge of the debt previously incurred; and our identification of ourselves in will with this new humanity enables us to accomplish that which was beyond us to accomplish so long as we were unconverted, with our lives directed otherwise than toward the fulfilment of the moral law. Kant does not so much exclude the actual or even necessary co-operation of divine grace with our own efforts in this new life as insist that we have nothing to do with that co-operation except to *deserve* it by making ourselves all the efforts that we can.

We may have to allow that what we may find to be an advantage possessed by Pascal's view over Kant's was due in part to his failure to realize some things of which Kant was better aware than he—such as the difficulty of finding genuine history in the early chapters of Genesis, or that of finding in the story there told, even if it were historically true, an explanation (as distinct from a symbol) of those facts of moral and religious experience for which it was supposed to account. Yet he may acknowledge that, here as on other occasions, Kant's view is chargeable with being abstract and unhistorical to an extreme degree, and that in these respects Pascal's is less open to criticism than his.

That our proper attitude towards divine grace is that, indicated by Kant, of seeking to deserve it by doing our duty to the utmost rather than by an indolent waiting for divine assistance or an anxious attempt (exposed, as such an attempt always is, to the danger of self-delusion) to disentangle in our moral life the part played by God's grace from that which is traceable to our will or to our character and circumstances—this I do not question. But in order to accept Kant's teaching in this respect it is not necessary to forget that the consciousness of a reconciliation with God through union with an ideal of moral perfection as that which would solve the problem presented by man's dissatisfaction with his actual condition is itself historically mediated through the Christian Gospel of Christ's atonement for our sins, and that even the dissatisfaction with our actual condition which presents the problem is historically mediated not by a law recognized from the first as purely moral, but by a law 'contained' (to quote St. Paul) 'in ordinances'.[1] Nor is it necessary to ignore the actual presence in the historical community of which we find ourselves members

[1] Eph. ii. 15.

of a 'grace', to be indeed appropriated by us through a faith which is manifested in a good will operative in good works, but proceeding from an historical personality ('grace and truth', as the Fourth Gospel says,[1] 'came by Jesus Christ') and mediated to the individual through Scripture and tradition, sacrament and example. Pascal's joyful surrender of himself to the historical Mediator and to the living Church which is his 'body', the vehicle and organ of his abiding Spirit, gives to his religion a quality which one misses in Kant's, with its meticulous shrinking from the concrete and the historical which yet does not hinder his recoil upon the history—which *as history* he rejects—to supply him with the symbolism without which he cannot set forth the abstract truths he is endeavouring to enforce.

A later philosophy which (like other and very different post-Kantian philosophies) traces its descent from Kant has endeavoured to redress the balance and to see in history not, as Kant tended to do, a more convenient though inadequate symbol, but the actual life and process of the eternal Idea. In so doing it can use more readily than Kant the language of such a Christianity as Pascal's, for which God was actually incarnate and is really present in the life of his Church, and not (as for Kant, at least in the works published in his lifetime) an ideal to be acted upon, but neither contemplated as revealed, nor approached as capable of a personal relation with his worshipper.

[1] John i. 17.

Yet in this *rapprochement* with a religion such as Pascal's the philosophy of Absolute Idealism has sometimes moved away from the position which was the starting-point of both Pascal's and Kant's theories of religion. They have identified original sin with the finitude which distinguishes man from God; and, by reckoning sins among the 'hazards' incident to finitude, have approximated to Voltaire's view that man, like the rest of nature, is 'what he ought to be': namely, a *finite* being, not the infinite God; so that his imperfections are no enigma or paradox, as Pascal considers them, but just what one would expect in a being occupying the place which he occupies in the scheme of things. It is important, however, to notice where, notwithstanding this *rapprochement* between Voltaire's view and that of the Absolute Idealists, these differ from the great representative of the French *Aufklärung*; and where on the other hand they part company with Pascal, and (I think) with Kant also, notwithstanding that they would claim to stand rather with these than with Voltaire in their recognition of the superiority of a *religious* to a *naturalistic* ethic.

The type of thought which I am calling, in order to give it a name, Absolute Idealism does unquestionably differ widely in tone and temper from such a Naturalism as Voltaire's. Pascal's view of human nature as a riddle and a paradox, Kant's affirmation of a radical evil in it, would be acknowledged by them as showing a deeper insight than the

complacency of Voltaire's assertion that, like everything else in nature, man is what he ought to be. In
our consciousness of a disproportion between our
ideal and our reality—with all the sadness that it
brings—the sadness of which Shelley says: [1]

> We look before and after,
> And pine for what is not;
> Our sincerest laughter
> With some pain is fraught;

Our sweetest songs are those that tell of saddest thought
—in that consciousness this school recognizes precisely what is highest and most precious in our
humanity, that which in the language of religion is
called our consciousness of God. Our 'divine dis-
content' is not a vain refusal to be content with our
place in nature; it is the hall-mark of our being in
a genuine sense above everything else in nature; not
a mere finite being like the rest, but a finite being in
whom the Infinite, as falling short of which alone
does anything come to be called finite, is manifested
or incarnate. The sense of alienation from God
which Pascal felt so deeply and expressed in such
memorable language is no illusion; it is the natural
attendant of our awakening from the state of being
finite indeed but having no thought of the Infinite,
being in no way aware of it, still less troubled by it,
into that awareness of the Infinite which discovers to
us our own imperfection and brings with it the sense
of a guilt due not to what we have done but to what
we *are*. In the same way the atonement wrought for

[1] *To a Skylark.*

us by Jesus Christ, through faith in which Pascal found himself enabled to overcome this sense of alienation, is no mere fable. In the spirit of the interpretation already, as we have seen, given by Kant to this article of the Christian creed, we can recognize this Atonement in our identification of ourselves not with our finitude and imperfection as individuals, but with that divine life which is ever transforming humanity in those human beings who yield themselves up to it in unselfish devotion to causes which transcend their individual desires and interests; a self-surrender which has found its pattern and its inspiration in the example and teaching of One whose meat was to do the will of him that sent him, and left himself no will but that higher will, although it meant for him the cup of suffering and death. Thus can Absolute Idealism accept the religion of Pascal, its sorrow and its joy, not as foolishness but as the perception, even if in a figure, of eternal truth. And by such acceptance it contrasts strongly with Voltaire's impatient rejection of that religion as a wilful and gratuitous misinterpretation of facts in which good sense finds nothing to wonder at. It may even be said to reverse Voltaire's position. For that rests upon the assumption that what is ought to be: that 'whatever is', in Pope's famous summary of the creed of eighteenth century deism, 'is right'.[1] The position of Absolute Idealism is, as I say, the reverse of this: namely that what ought to

---

[1] *Essay on Man*, Ep. iv.

be *is*, in a deeper and truer significance of the word than that of an existence obvious to the outward senses; and that it is precisely the characteristic insight of *Religion* that this is so. Kant, it is held, was unduly timorous in his refusal to allow that such religious faith could claim the name of knowledge.

'All unsatisfied endeavour ceases', says Hegel, 'when we learn that the final purpose of the world is accomplished no less than ever accomplishing itself. Generally speaking, this is the belief and attitude of the man; while the young imagine that the world is utterly sunk in wickedness, and that the first thing needful is to change it into something else. The religious mind, on the contrary, views the world as ruled by Divine Providence, and therefore correspondent with what it ought to be.' [1]

Now, before going on to ask whether, in this presentation by Absolute Idealism of the true nature of Religion, something is not lost which Pascal and Kant retained, and the retention of which hindered the latter and would have hindered the former, had Absolute Idealism come within the ken of his thought, from taking the step which it demands, let us recognize that Religion *does* stand for the conviction that the Good is no mere aspiration or unrealized—perhaps unrealizable—ideal but the ultimate Reality behind all appearances whatever. Implicit in all monotheism, such as Pascal's, and explicitly acknowledged by Kant in an awkward form, when he reasons to

[1] *Encycl., Die Logik,* § 234; *Werke*, vi, p. 407; tr. Wallace, *Logic of Hegel,* p. 323.

the existence of God as postulated by the 'manifest authority' (as Butler calls it) of the moral law, this conviction is precisely what delivers the religious believer from the perplexities and dubieties which beset those to whom the voice of conscience does not indeed speak in vain, but appears to be, for all its unmistakable claim upon our obedience, as it were crying in the wilderness of an alien world. For the *moral* consciousness the Good is at the most what Kant called a categorical imperative, an unconditional 'ought'; for the *religious* consciousness it is the supreme and ultimate reality.

If this be so, it is clear that, for religion, the evil and imperfection which we find in the world must be in the last resort held to be embraced within and subordinated to an order itself perfect and good; and such an inclusion and subordination is certainly most easily envisaged if we regard certain aspects of moral and religious experience as in fact illusory. What I have in mind is the clear distinction which we make in our moral judgement of ourselves between a *fault*, committed where we could have done otherwise, for which we blame ourselves and feel remorse, and a *defect*, due to inherited disability or to circumstances over which we have no control, for which we do *not* blame ourselves, and for which we do not feel *remorse*, although we may quite possibly feel a *resentment* against our lot in suffering from such a defect as bitter as any *remorse* for a fault which we impute to ourselves. If our *faults* are in the end due merely to our finitude, though it may be possible to show reason why they appear to us different from such *defects* as I have contrasted with them, yet in the long run, from a point of view to which in philosophy we, or some of us, can rise, *remorse* for them must appear something as inappropriate in their case as in that of such defects.

So much for *moral* experience as distinguished from *religious*. But in religious experience also Absolute Idealism claims to lift us to a point of view from which that personal relation to God which is the presupposition of so much of our religious experience—and with it the significance of *sin* as transgression of the divine will—must come to be regarded as only a figure or metaphor of what is, philosophically considered, something quite other than this. Although the philosophical account given of that which is symbolized by religious worship may not be quite the same in all absolute idealists— not the same in Hegel as in Gentile, in the late Mr. Bosanquet as in Mr. Collingwood, yet I think it true to say that, according to all alike, it is possible for us to attain an insight for which the personal relation between God and man is apprehended, not only as something which is inadequately regarded when described in terms appropriate to the social relation between two finite beings, but as in its truth not a personal relation at all, because it is (to use terms often employed in this connexion) one of 'pure immanence' in which there is no genuine 'transcendence' left at all. Now I desire to suggest that this transformation of such a moral and religious experience as we find exemplified in every line of the author we are now studying is *not* one which leaves intact its essential nature and value; and secondly that, as I have attempted to argue at greater length than I can here allow myself,[1] Absolute Idealism does not to my mind succeed in its treatment of the individual personality, the 'finite centre of experience' (to use Bradley's phrase) apart from which we know nothing of 'experience', 'idea', or 'spirit' at all. The question really at issue between the absolute idealist's interpretation of moral and religious experience and that of such a writer as Pascal or (I think I may add) as Kant, is the question of the standing in reality to be assigned to the individual personality.

VIII

PASCAL ON PERSONALITY

BUT here those who have so far followed me may very reasonably raise the following difficulty. Granted that moral and religious experience postulate the reality of the individual person and of a personal relation borne by him to God; that, if these are not real, the consciousness of sin and of the sinner's reconciliation with God become illusory,

[1] In the ninth of my second series of Gifford Lectures, published under the title of *Divine Personality and Human Life*.

have we not ourselves advanced some considerable way towards what we are thus considering as a dissipation of moral and religious experience into a phantasmagoria by our doctrine of Original Sin, on which (as we have seen) both Pascal and Kant lay so much stress? For Original Sin seems to be just the sin which we do not impute to the individual person, nor the individual person to himself, as his own free act; but the sin which he finds himself as it were entangled in, depriving him of that freedom to do what he sees to be right which he would fain claim to be an (or even *the*) essential attribute of Personality. It would take us too far aside from our main subject to follow up now the conception of Original Sin; but we may perhaps make the two following observations:

1. It is true that the doctrine of Original Sin *is* inconsistent with a *crude* individualism in theology, since it recognizes that the individual person does not in fact stand alone; that he is, to the roots of his spiritual nature, a *social* being—just as the doctrine of the Trinity corrects an error, which might arise from taking the consciousness of a personal relation with God in religion in too naïve a manner, by recognizing that God cannot ultimately be conceived as *a* person side by side, so to say, with finite persons.

2. Nevertheless it is only the individual consciousness of sin that gives significance to those facts of moral experience which demand a doctrine of

Original Sin to account for them; just as, although we find ourselves proud or ashamed (as the case may be) of actions which are those of our nation, although we as individuals had no part in the performance of them, this consciousness is only known as what it is because we know what it is to be ashamed or proud of acts *as our own*, and so we come to be puzzled when we feel entitled from one point of view to *disown* acts whereof we are thus ashamed or proud. Thus I do not consider that the acceptance of a doctrine of Original Sin should be considered as the surrender of the claim which we make for the consciousness of individual personality to be taken more seriously than it is taken by most, if not by all, of the various forms which Absolute Idealism has assumed; a claim which is, I think, indissolubly connected with the claim of Religion to be an autonomous form of experience, not capable of being resolved without remainder into Philosophy. The two eminent thinkers whose work has within the last few years brought Italy to the front in philosophy, Croce and Gentile, differ, it is true, widely from each other in their attitude toward Religion. For Croce it is a mere immature, misunderstood form of Philosophy; for Gentile it is an essential stage in our spiritual development. Yet for both it is in the end to the philosopher who reflects upon it quite other than it seems while we are practising it; the God before whose majesty we abase ourselves, or to whose love we surrender ourselves, is known by the philosopher to be in fact our own spiritual nature objectified. The only true God, as Croce declares,[1] is *Deus in nobis* ET NOS; he is, to use language which is familiar to modern theologians, wholly *immanent* and not *transcendent* at all.

The late Baron Friedrich von Hügel was a specially earnest champion of the necessity to a vital and fruitful religion of the recognition of a genuine *transcendence* in its conception of God, and that not merely as a moment or factor in a process wherein, when contemplated by philosophy in its entirety, the appearance of transcendence should be found to have vanished, but as ultimate and irresolvable.

Nowhere, I think, will one find the case against immanentism put with greater force than by von Hügel; and that all the more that, unlike other critics of it, he had a profound knowledge of and sympathy with mysticism, and its aspiration after a realization in consciousness of the mystic's unity with his God. But in von Hügel his protest against sheer immanentism was intimately connected with his doctrine of two levels of finite or creaturely spiritual life, in the tension and resultant harmony between which alone it could reach its appointed end. Pascal, as one would expect from Sainte-Beuve's description of him, already cited, as *l'esprit le moins panthéistique qu'on puisse concevoir*, was certainly no sheer 'immanentist' in his theology; and his doctrine, derived from St. Augustine, of the two-fold love

[1] *Saggio sullo Hegel* (ed. 1913), p. 137 (Eng. tr. p. 201).

natural to man, of God and of self, is closely related to the 'two-level' theory which we find so constantly urged by von Hügel. There was, however, a strain of thought in Pascal, which, proceeding from a principle other than that which usually conducts to *immanentism*, yet led to a result which is, in von Hügel's view, if less prejudicial than immanentism, no less certainly prejudicial to the true balance and health of our spiritual life—namely the denial of real and relatively independent value to any other spiritual activities than that which is expressly religious or God-directed.

'God has made man with two loves—one for God, the other for self—with this law, however, that our love for God should be infinite, that is without any end but God himself; but our self-love finite, and leading beyond ourselves to God.' So Pascal states the doctrine in his letter to his sister Mme Périer on the death of their father.[1] Presumably no Christian would dispute this. But a Christian ought in the first place to inquire whether, without contradicting, it yet did not differ from the doctrine of the New Testament in its silence about the love of one's neighbour. True, we are taught in the Gospel to love our neighbours as ourselves; and this presupposes a love of self. But in Pascal's treatment of the matter, even though he is actually engaged in consoling a sister under a stroke of bereavement, one finds a very decided tendency to regard the love of our

[1] p. 102.

neighbour as swallowed up in that of God. We did not love our father, he tells Mme Périer for the first time at his death; from his dedication to God in his baptism he belonged to God, not to his children. I think we shall find in many of Pascal's utterances a tone in this matter which contrasts very sharply both with that either of the Gospel declaration, that what is done to the least of Christ's brethren is done to himself,[1] and with the teaching of the First Epistle of St. John that by dwelling in the love of the brethren we dwell in the God who is love.[2] I do not mean to say that Pascal's piety was not in accord with that which these New Testament texts would suggest. On the contrary, we find him profoundly moved by the former, so that even when he was dying and the doctors did not allow him to receive the Sacrament, he begged to have a poor sick man brought to share the care which was being bestowed upon himself: 'Ne pouvant pas communier dans le chef, je voudrais bien communier dans ses membres.'[3] But in his writings I do not think it can be denied that we shall find a decided tendency to disparage the value of our natural affection for those most closely connected with ourselves, since no finite being can be regarded as 'end' to any other: God alone is the sole end of all. The contrast with Kant's insistence on the importance of looking on all rational beings as 'ends in themselves' is striking; though it might be possible to show that there is,

[1] Matt. xxv. 40. [2] 1 John iv. 16. [3] *Vie*, p. 38.

when the contexts are considered, no contradiction between the statements of the two. Pascal would not justify treating another person as a mere means to any purpose of our own, and Kant conceived of the persons who, as such, are ends in themselves as forming a society the mutual relations of whose members are determined altogether by one and the same divine law. Moreover, that to which Pascal is concerned to deny what he thinks are dangerously excessive claims is not our practical love for all those who are as much ends in themselves as we, but our individual affections for our own kindred and friends; while Kant also insists that the love of our neighbour which has moral worth is just not this 'pathological' love as he calls it—not in the modern sense of 'morbid', but in that of 'emotional'—but the practical good will which we are bound to show to any man, enemy as well as friend, stranger as well as intimate. Pascal's one end for all and Kant's one law for all come to much the same; and while to both the natural affections seem apt to conflict with the demand of reason based on the equality of all men before God and the moral law, Pascal allows to our emotions an outlet, which Kant is unwilling to consider legitimate, in personal devotion to God, especially as revealed to us in Jesus Christ.

Neither Kant nor Pascal find any great worth in our affections for particular individuals. They seem to the one to belong to a region lower than that at which reason presents to every being capable of

apprehending a law of universal obligation; to the
other to be apt to divert from its proper object the
love due from us to God alone. It is characteristic
of von Hügel that he quite definitely finds in his
doctrine of 'two levels' a point of view from which
he at once can recognize that most of us are right
in valuing very highly our special attachments, and
also that there may be, as the Christian Church from
the days of its Founder downward has ever taught,
a call to some to renounce them and devote themselves exclusively to the cultivation of the love of
God. But von Hügel's attitude would hardly have
satisfied Pascal. Pascal seems to require of every
Christian an indifference or even an aversion to all
which is desirable to ordinary human nature. In a
fallen man even the instinctive love of self has
become irrational. The 'moi' in us is *hateful*.[1] He
cannot overlook the plain statement of the New
Testament that Christ did not seek the cup of
suffering but prayed that it might pass from him.
But he explains away any inference which might be
drawn from this as to what is proper for us by
drawing a distinction between Christ's sinless and
unfallen humanity and our own. *He* was right in
loving his self, but *we* are not.[2] It is sufficient to say
that there is no shadow of support in the New
Testament for making Christ's example to be no
example for us just where it has been most precious

[1] *P.* § 455, p. 541.　　　[2] *Lettre à Mme. Périer sur la mort de
leur père*, pp. 102, 103.

to those who have found in it proof of his sympathy with trials the very bitterness of which consists in this, that we are called to surrender *not* what is bad and hateful but what we rightly cherish and love. Nor again is there any support there for the strange saying that 'sickness is the natural state for a Christian',[1] a saying which is surely itself nothing less than morbid, and deserving still more than those which immediately occasioned the exclamation which I have already quoted from Voltaire: 'Hélas, encore hélas, Pascal; on voit bien que vous êtes malade!'

So far from this attitude of Pascal's being characteristically Christian, as he would appear to have thought it to be, it seems to belong rather to a type of asceticism which has indeed often figured as Christian, but whose descent is to be traced rather to the philosophy of the Cynics and the Stoics than to the New Testament. The topics of the contemptibleness of human nature, the loathsomeness of the human body in many of its functions when alive and in the process of its inevitable decay after death, of the triviality of everyday bereavements—these have been common enough in Christian devotional literature from the *Collations* of Cassian to the *Holy Dying* of Jeremy Taylor; but those who dwell upon them must seek their models elsewhere than in the New Testament; and it is easy enough to find such in the literature of Stoicism. It is remarkable that

[1] *Vie*, p. 37.

when Shakespeare, of whom one is sometimes tempted to say that the Christian religion is the one thing
he did not understand, wishes to put into the mouth
of the disguised Duke in *Measure for Measure*[1] the
consolations which a Christian priest might be
supposed to offer to a dying man condemned to
death, in order to win him to pious resignation to
his inevitable doom, the reflections which he makes
him urge are all of this purely Stoical type; and it is
with a sense of incongruity that we find the mere
disgust with life which they have instilled into
Claudio apparently regarded as the proper frame
of mind in which a Christian should meet his end.
It is a fact of historical importance that when the
Christian Church emerged on to the stage of Graeco-
Roman civilization, as it took the Platonic philosophy for its metaphysical so it took the Stoic
philosophy for its ethical background. With the
perception of a certain kinship in spirit between
Seneca and St. Paul, which gave rise to the very
old legend of their friendship and correspondence,
went an incorporation into the literary tradition of
Christian ascetic piety of a strain of disparagement
of the body scarcely congruous with the doctrine of
the Incarnation, and suggesting a different type of
self-denial from that implied in the gospel sayings
about plucking out the eye and cutting off the hand,
where what is sacrificed is plainly intended to be

[1] Act. 3. sc. 1. Cp. *Hibbert Journal*, Jan. 1928, art. on 'Shakespeare and Religion'.

regarded not as something bad or contemptible but as something good and precious.

Pascal, as we have seen, justifies his adoption of the principle of the *hatefulness* of the self as the motive for asceticism by his doctrine of the corruption of human nature by the fall; so that, whereas Adam in Paradise or Jesus Christ could rightly *love* their selves, *we* cannot. But it is, I think, quite impossible to follow him in representing this as the genuinely Christian view. The love of our neighbour is prescribed in the New Testament on the presupposition of a love of self which is obviously considered as natural and blameless; and even St. Paul, whose passionate expressions in the Epistle to the Romans ('I know that in me, that is, in my flesh, dwelleth no good thing' [1]) lie behind the Augustinian theology which Pascal adopted and perhaps, like the Jansenists with whom he sympathized, exaggerated—even St. Paul elsewhere declares, in a context which makes it plain that he is not censuring the natural disposition which he describes: 'No man ever yet hated his own flesh, but nourisheth and cherisheth it.' [2] It is true that the authorship of the Epistle whence these words are quoted—the Epistle to the Ephesians—is less unquestionably Pauline than that to the Romans; but Pascal at any rate would not have discriminated between them as evidence of the Apostle's mind. I think then that we may justly consider Pascal's basing of his asceticism on the *hatefulness* of

[1] Rom. vii. 18.　　　　[2] Eph. v. 29.

the self to be a deviation from the principle which distinguishes the properly *Christian* asceticism—the principle which does not deny but rather insists upon the *goodness*—not merely the pleasantness or attractiveness, but the *goodness*—of what is surrendered for the sake of something yet *better*.

IX

PASCAL ON GRACE

I TURN now to another distinctive feature of Pascal's philosophy of religion. That philosophy, as we have seen, was not systematic, so that we can only treat it by calling attention to its main characteristics and indicating their connexion with each other. We have seen in Pascal's doctrine of the *hatefulness* of self what one may call the darker, or, if we like to use the expression, the pessimistic side of his view; this is, however, compensated by a strong emphasis on the *love* of God as the very essence of the Christian—that is, for Pascal, of the true and final—religion. In his insistence on this point he was specially concerned to combat certain errors, as he held them to be, in the presentation of Christianity by the influential Jesuits of his day, and it will be interesting and instructive to show how he stood over against these teachers in the matter. For while Pascal unquestionably conceived of them as taking the heart of joy out of Christianity by allowing that one could be a Christian without loving God, they, on the other hand, were in fact concerned not to make it a gloomy religion but rather to temper it to weak brethren by minimizing its demands on the inner man and concentrating on the outward profession and conformity which would keep within the circle of religious influences men who would otherwise be lost altogether to the Church and to religion.

The true religion, says Pascal, consists solely in the love of God.[1] This being so, he can find nothing of genuine religious value in the presentation of Christianity which entertains the possibility that the salvation which it promises is to be obtained without such love really present in the heart. He speaks with indignation of carnal Christians who seem to hold that Christ came to dispense us from exercising that love of God which had been the only truly acceptable part even of the religion of the Old Testament, and to 'give us the sacraments, which do all that is required without our co-operation'.[2] Pascal's seriousness in this view is not fully grasped if we forget that he did not merely acquiesce in but zealously accepted the Roman Church's doctrine of the sacraments; any hesitation to believe in the dogma of transubstantiation in the Eucharist moved him not only to opposition but to impatience.[3] Thus he was not thinking of the sacraments as a Protestant

[1] P. § 610, p. 601.　　　　[2] See P. § 224, p. 451.
　　　　[3] P. § 607, p. 600.

using the like words might do, as, however venerable from their associations, yet mere outward cere-
monies, which may indeed express or symbolize the
feelings and dispositions of a religious man, but
which are nevertheless without any objective efficacy
of their own. He had no intention, we may be sure,
of contradicting the declaration of the Council of
Trent [1] that they confer grace *ex opere operato*. Yet he
revolted against any theory which, under the sem-
blance of exalting sacramental grace, tended to sub-
stitute a religion which like 'carnal Judaism' considered membership of the chosen people—though
this be, for Christians, membership, not through
physical descent, but through sacramental incorporation—the main matter on which salvation depends,
and personal love of God a grace reserved only for
a few favoured saints.

The history of Christendom is full of controversies
arising from tension between the enthusiasm which
refuses to purchase the chance of permeating human
society at the price of lowering its witness to a high
standard of personal religion and the passion for
souls which refuses to abandon altogether even the
weakest and most erring of the flock while it is in
any way possible to keep them within hearing of the
Shepherd's voice. Neither side has lacked its saintly
champions; both can appeal to words of Christ
himself. The one is exposed to the temptation to
narrowness, spiritual pride, exorbitant pretensions;

[1] Sess. vii, Can. 8.

the other to the temptation to covet popularity and power and to accommodate principles to the practice of the world. In Pascal's day the one side was represented by the Jansenists, the other by the Jesuits; and Pascal on this moral issue was heart and soul with the Jansenists. As with the opposition offered by the Montanists to the Catholicism of the Roman Bishops of the second and third centuries, so with the opposition of the Jansenists to the dominant party in the Roman Catholic Church of the seventeenth; it attracted to itself some of the holiest and most intelligent spirits of the time, and its protest exerted a bracing and purifying influence on the life of the Church; yet its complete or formal triumph would not have been in the Church's true interest; although this is not to say that it would not have been in that interest to welcome and listen to its warnings rather than meet it with disparagement and persecution. On the tension between the factors in religious life for which these contending parties stood the health and permanence of that life at all times depends; and the problem for each generation is to maintain the balance between them in such a manner that each should not neutralize the other, but that each should, with the other's good will, make to the full its positive contribution to the activity of the whole community.

The controversy about grace to which so much of the *Lettres Provinciales* of our author is devoted is not in its details of any great importance for the

understanding of his philosophy of religion. He was
concerned in it not because he was interested from
the point of view of a dogmatic theologian in the
distinctions between the different kinds of grace
recognized by writers on the subject, but because
he thought that the Jesuit teaching was dangerous
to morality and disgraceful to religion, of which the
Jesuits were in the eyes of their many penitents the
representatives.

But here again, if we attempt to penetrate the
moral and religious significance of the questions at
issue between the Jesuits and Pascal, we shall find
it requires no less delicate a discrimination to state it
exactly than does the matter of the love of God.

The mysterious problem which gave rise to the
whole discussion is that of the relation of the grace
of God to the free will of man. The 'doctor of grace',
St. Augustine, had maintained against Pelagius and
his followers the necessity of divine grace to originate
every good action of man in his fallen state, in which
the free will with which the first man was created
is crippled, and is (apart from a special act of God)
incapable of originating a *good*, though not incapable
of originating a *bad* action. He did not deny the
existence of free will even in fallen man; but very
little scope was left to it by his combination of the
view that it was only free to originate bad actions
with a strong stress upon the doctrine of the predestination to salvation by an inscrutable decree of
a few elect persons out of the 'mass of sin' in which

the majority of the descendants of Adam were left to incur the eternal punishment due to that sin; although in them (as in the case of infants who die unbaptized) it might be only original and not actual, that is individual, sin at all. This doctrine of Augustine, which could appeal to texts of St. Paul in its favour and especially to some in the Epistle to the Romans, was never repudiated by the Church; while to the western Church Augustine became, to a degree incomparably greater than any other of the Fathers, the oracle of its theology. Thus in the *Sentences* of Peter Lombard, which in the Middle Ages was the theological text-book of the Universities and the subject of commentary by every principal Schoolman, the extracts from Augustine enormously outnumber those from any other authority. Yet the Council of Orange, held in A.D. 529, a century after Augustine's death, in reaffirming Augustine's doctrine had reaffirmed it in a form which dropped from it the extreme predestinarianism to which he had sometimes committed himself, and anathematized the assertion that any persons are predestined to evil by divine power. Towards the end of the Middle Ages there was a marked tendency to emphasize the freedom of the will, a tendency which brought about a reaction at the Reformation, issuing in Luther's assertion that the will of fallen man is a *servum*, not a *liberum arbitrium*, and in the unmitigated predestinarianism of Calvin. This reaction inevitably disposed the teachers of the Counter-Reformation,

and especially the Jesuits, who were the heart and
soul of that movement, to a reassertion of the liberty
in human nature which the Reformers had denied—
a reassertion which in its turn led to a revolt on the
part of those whose religious experiences, cast in the
mould of that of St. Paul and St. Augustine, had
inspired them with a specially vivid sense of their
utter dependence upon God from first to last,
against what seemed to them to be a tendency to
whittle away the necessity of grace prevenient,
efficacious, irresistible, to enable a man to begin,
continue, and end a life of deeds acceptable to God
and leading to ultimate salvation.   Such persons
turned back from the Jesuit theology of their day to
the great Doctor whom the Church professed to
venerate beyond all teachers outside the sacred circle
of those whose writings were included in Holy
Scripture; and their views found expression in *Augustinus*, the famous book of Jansenius, Bishop of
Ypres, in which he attempted to set forth the true
and unadulterated doctrine of him whom, as Pascal says, 'the Popes and the Church have given us
as our guide in these matters'.   The Abbé St.-Cyran,
who had been the confessor of the nuns of Port-
Royal, was a personal friend of Jansenius, and the
circle of religious and educated men who stood in
an intimate relation to that house—a circle which
included Arnauld, nephew of the Mère Angélique,
the abbess to whom the reform of the convent was
due, and Pascal, whose sister was a nun in it—were

sympathetic with the Augustinianism of which the Dutch theologian was the spokesman, though not all could be called Jansenists. Pascal certainly would not have accepted the name.[1] But he was a devout admirer of St. Augustine and, like him, so profoundly conscious of dependence upon divine grace for all that was good in him that he would sympathize with Jansenist jealousy of any view which seemed to detract from its sovereignty, as the doctrine of some of the Jesuit doctors of his time seemed to him and to his friends certainly to do. But, after dealing in the first three letters of the series known as *Les Lettres Provinciales* with some of the sophistries, as they appeared to him, about 'sufficient and actual grace' in which the Jesuit controversialists indulged —and even in respect of these he nowhere passes to the consideration of the deeper theological questions which gave rise to these sophistries—he turns aside to the more congenial task of exposing the injury to morality which could be charged against the ingenious casuistry of the fashionable Jesuit writers on moral theology. This fact indicates, I think, no very intense interest in the speculative problems of grace and free will, and suggests that he was engaged upon one side in the discussion chiefly by his sympathy with the moral and religious temper of that side as compared with that of the other.

It was less, I think, the Jesuit championship of the freedom of the will than their readiness to con-

[1] See *P.* § 865, p. 731.

template the possibility of a Christianity from which the love of God was absent that roused Pascal's indignation. Indeed it might be contended that he thought the Jesuits attributed too much to one kind of grace—or perhaps we should say, to grace mediated in one kind of way—when they encouraged, as he thought they did, contentment with a level of Christian life and conduct in which, relying on the efficacy of the grace received through participation in the sacraments of the Church, one did not aspire to a personal love of God and to the self-devotion which such a love must inevitably, in proportion to its reality and depth, inspire in those whom it animated.

It was the central thought of Pascal's philosophy of religion that the essential function of religion, by its discharge of which the validity of any religious system must be tested, was to be found in the cultivation and expression of *love*, that is, of divine love, directed to the one all-satisfying object, namely God, and to our brethren in him. The most elaborate expression of this thought is perhaps to be found in a passage wherein he speaks of *la charité* as follows[1]:

'The infinite distance which separates bodies from

---

[1] This word of course is the regular traditional translation of ἀγαπή, the word which, doubtless on account of its complete, or almost complete, freedom from association with sexual love, is appropriated in the New Testament to that specifically Christian sentiment of love to God and man which is glorified in the thirteenth chapter of St. Paul's first Epistle to the Corinthians and in the first of the Epistles ascribed to St. John.

minds is a figure of that distance, infinitely more infinite, which separates minds from charity, for this latter distance belongs to the supernatural order. All the glory of worldly greatness has no splendour in the eyes of those who are occupied in the things of the mind; while the greatness of the men of mind is invisible to kings, rich men, military chieftains, and all those who are great after the flesh. The greatness of that sole true wisdom which is from God is in its turn invisible both to the men of the flesh and to those of mind. Here we have three orders which differ in kind from one another. The men of great genius have their dominion, their glory, their greatness, their victory, their splendour, and have no need of the trappings of material greatness, with which they have nothing to do. They are perceived not with the bodily eyes but with the mind, and that is enough for them. The Saints have their empire, their glory, their victory, their splendour, and they have no need of those sorts of greatness which belong to the flesh or to the mind, with which they have nothing to do, and which neither add anything to them nor take anything from them. They are perceived by God and by the angels and not by the bodily senses or by inquisitive minds; and God is enough for them.

'Archimedes, without any external glory, would be none the less esteemed. He did not win spectacular battles, but he has enriched all minds by his discoveries. How great is his glory in the realm of mind!

'Jesus Christ, without worldly wealth and without having any fruits of knowledge to show, is to be ranked in the order of holiness. He made no discoveries, he exercised no dominion, but he was humble, patient, holy,

holy in the sight of God, terrible to evil spirits, free from all sin. How great the splendour, how wonderful the magnificence of his coming in the eyes of the heart which can apprehend wisdom !

'Even if Archimedes had been a prince, there would have been no advantage in his giving himself the airs of one in his books on mathematics. There would have been no advantage to our Lord Jesus Christ, as regards glory in that sphere of holiness wherein he is sovereign, to come as a king; but assuredly he came with the glory appropriate to the order to which he belongs.

'It is very idle to be offended by the low estate in which Jesus Christ was born, as though this low estate were low in the same order of values to which belongs the kind of greatness which he came to display. If one considers this latter greatness as shown in his life, in his sufferings, in his obscurity, in his death, in his choice of his disciples, in his desertion by them, in his secret resurrection, and so on, one will find that greatness so great that one will have no occasion to be offended by a lowness which is not there.

'But there are some who can admire nothing but fleshly greatness, as though there were no greatness of the mind; and others who only admire that of the mind, as though there were not infinitely higher kinds of greatness to be found in wisdom.

'All the material objects in the world, the firmament, the stars, the earth and its kingdoms, are not equal in value to the least of minds; for the mind *knows* all that and itself as well; while material objects know nothing.

'All material objects taken together, and all minds taken together and all their works are not equal in value to the least motion of charity; for such a movement belongs to an order of things infinitely more exalted than either the material or the mental. Out of all the material objects in the world taken together one could not produce one little thought; that is impossible, for thought belongs to a different order of objects altogether. From all bodies and minds taken together one could not derive one motion of true charity; that is impossible; it belongs to another order, the supernatural.'[1]

Of this celebrated passage Voltaire has remarked[2] that 'one may well believe that M. Pascal would not have included this rigmarole in his work, if he had had time to revise it'.

Now here, as elsewhere, we find Voltaire unappreciative of that spiritual passion in Pascal which so often lies behind his utterances, even where we may hold with his critic that the reasoning suggested would not bear too close a scrutiny; but I do not think we can resist agreeing with the latter that it would have been well to reconsider the terms in which he has here expressed himself.

One need not perhaps dwell upon the illusory air of mathematical precision introduced by the use of the words 'infinitely infinite' in the first sentence, as though one were dealing with infinities, of different orders indeed, but all nevertheless susceptible of mathematical treatment, whereas this is not here the case, since the first-mentioned *distance*, that

[1] § 793, pp. 695 ff.   [2] Œuvres, t. 22, p. 39.

between bodies and minds, is of course purely meta-
phorical, and this again is said to be only a 'figure'
of the 'distance' between minds and charity. At the
same time it is difficult not to feel that the attraction
of the mathematical metaphor to the mathematician
in Pascal lay to some degree in its hint of a certain
exactitude of conception in the thought which the
mathematical metaphor was used to elucidate;
whereas it is very difficult to convince oneself that
his language here has in fact by any means the
exactitude appropriate to a philosophical subject.

In the first place the disparateness upon which
Pascal insists as existing between 'bodies' (that
is, material things) and *pensées* (facts of consciousness)—a disparateness which of course was a familiar theme in the age of Descartes, in whose philosophy it occupied so prominent a place, and gave
rise to the peculiar difficulty which the Cartesians
found in the apparent interaction of mind and body
in man—this disparateness is essentially a disparateness between bodies, merely as such—things extended
in space—and what we may call facts of consciousness,
as such, and whatever we may think is required to
account for these. The moment that one substitutes
for bodies, as such, bodies regarded as organic to consciousness and thought, you have left the disparateness behind and jumped, so to say, the problems
which it raises. Yet this Pascal does when he
assigns the life of captains and kings and the glory
thereto belonging to the 'order of bodies'. Even when

he speaks of 'the firmament, the stars, the earth *and its kingdoms*' as belonging to the material order, one sees this confusion, as I think it is, creeping in. The division of the earth into kingdoms belongs to *political* geography; and only *physical* geography is relevant here. And though we may regard the thoughts of kings and captains and of 'men of the world' generally as directed to those forms of consciousness which are most obviously occasioned and conditioned by bodily movements, and may hold the speculations of the mathematician and the physicist, because concerned with characteristics of the extended world in abstraction from its sensible qualities, to be on this account less materialistic (we might nowadays, following Croce, prefer to call them less *economic*) than the preoccupations of the kings and captains—we are, even in dealing with worldly achievements and worldly estimates of value, dealing with *minds* and *thoughts*, and not with *bodies* considered as mere extended and moving objects. Then again if, forgetting this truth, as Pascal seems to forget it, we go on to the 'order of wisdom' or 'of charity'—he calls it by both names—it is obvious that we are still speaking of *thoughts* and *feelings*, not of *bodies* as mere extended and moving objects; so that however superior in value the saint may be to Archimedes and spiritual wisdom to science, the latter is plainly not removed from the former by the same absolute disparateness as lies between a body considered as a mere extended and moving object and (as

Pascal says) *une petite pensée*. If we try to think out this *Pensée* of Pascal's it turns out so unsatisfactory and inconsistent that one may excuse Voltaire, who, we said, did not sympathize with the passion behind it, calling it in his disrespectful way a *galimatias*.

It is the passion behind it which is important. The expression is—I am speaking of course of its argumentative force, not of its style—so unsatisfactory that it confirms the view to which I think a dispassionate study of the *Pensées* leads us, that Pascal was not only not a great philosopher in the sense in which Descartes and Kant were great philosophers, but that his greatness as a writer on religion is attributable to the genuineness and profundity of his religious experience combined with the wonderful artistry of his language; not, as is sometimes supposed, to the clearness and accuracy of his thought *about* that experience.

The passion behind the passage, in which we found it so hard to discover on analysis an intelligible argument, is that passionate love for God revealed in Jesus Christ, whom by this very capacity to seek him he knows he has already found; whom he hears speaking to him in the immortal words: *Console-toi, tu ne me chercherais pas si tu ne m'avais trouvé—tu ne me chercherais pas si tu ne me possédais. Ne t'inquiète donc pas.*[1]

In his ever-recurring insistence on the thought that God is, in the prophet's phrase, a God that

[1] §§ 553, 555, pp. 576, 578.

hideth himself, *un Dieu caché, Deus absconditus*, Pascal is a forerunner of many contemporaries of our own, among whom Rudolf Otto is perhaps at the moment the best known in this country. These are the spokesmen of an inevitable reaction. For a century there has prevailed among scholars, especially in Germany, a view which found either in morality or in the idealism whose motto was Hegel's saying,[1] 'What God is, that he imparts and reveals', the true substance of Religion. Now we have pressed upon us as of primary importance the mysterious—not to say irrational—factor present as well in the historic faith of Christendom as in the heathen superstition or Jewish ritualism with which it was customary to contrast it.

Those of whom I am thinking may find in Pascal a kindred point. For he has, as we have seen, no sympathy with what he calls *deism*, a religion of pure reason, relying on the argument from design in nature or on the eternity of truth as ascertained by the exact sciences. He does not deny that reason may lead us to a knowledge of God, but it is only to a knowledge 'useless and sterile', as he says,[2] apart from Jesus Christ. For a deep sense of sin and of our powerlessness to avoid it made it impossible for him to rest in deism. It is almost as far, he says, from true Christianity as atheism itself. When he thinks of the position in which man finds himself in regard to God apart from the Christian revelation, he thinks of him as confronted on the one hand by

[1] *Werke*, vi, pp. 277, 278.   [2] *P.* § 556, p. 581.

an incomprehensible infinity—a 'Being infinite and
without parts';[1] on the other by the wrath of God
manifested in our ineradicable consciousness of
guilt in the presence of the moral law—an 'irritated
God'[2] into whose hands, if death be not extinction,
we must then fall. Why, asked Voltaire,[3] need it be
an irritated God? Why not a good and merciful
God? But Pascal saw no evidence of divine love in
nature; and it is perhaps harder still to find evidence
of it there for us nowadays with our greatly extended
knowledge on the one hand of the inconceivable
vastness of a material universe, to all appearance
utterly indifferent to our desires and ideals, on the
other hand of the ruthless struggle for existence
among living beings of the same species and between
different species of living beings. And if the God
revealed in nature was incomprehensible and indifferent, the God revealed in conscience was an
offended God. Pascal was profoundly conscious of
not deserving any goodness or mercy at his hands.
He was one of those who are always penitent, to
whom—as I have heard another such say of himself—the text in *Lamentations*, 'It is of the Lord's
mercies that we are not consumed',[4] recurs every day
as the only adequate expression of their attitude
towards the Giver of the law which they know
themselves to be daily breaking. It was in Jesus
Christ and in him alone that he found the assurance

[1] P. § 233, p. 442.   [3] *Œuvres*, t. 31, p. 16.
[2] P. § 194, p. 419.   [4] Lam. iii. 22.

of God's love. Just as God was not so hidden in nature but that man could divine his existence—yet so hidden that only to those who had faith drawn from other sources was his existence certain, so Christ's claim to be what God is was sufficiently attested by prophecies and miracles for the satisfaction of those who are willing to be satisfied—insufficiently to satisfy those who are unwilling. The Christian revelation was thus analogous to God's revelation of himself apart from Christianity in its mixture of evidence and obscurity; but it surpassed it in its revelation of a divine love appealing for an unreserved and whole-hearted response.

We may find Pascal's apology for Christianity unconvincing in its exposition of the evidence from the Scriptural records of prophecy and miracle; and we are not likely to agree with him in finding in the healing of the abscess in the eye of his niece Marguerite Périer by the touch of what was believed to be a thorn from our Saviour's crown an overpowering proof that God's arm is not shortened since Bible days. But the real force of his apology still abides in the experience wherein Pascal is at one with Christians of all generations in finding the love of Christ sufficient to bring the assurance of deliverance from the power of sin even to those who are most sensible of their subjection to that power; and this without any lowering, but rather with a heightening of that moral ideal by their perception of which they have measured the depth of their own falling short of it; and in finding this love mediated to them through the historic tradition of Christian doctrine and worship, the abiding strength of which its survival of the destruction of many things that once seemed to be integral parts of it does but the more remarkably evince.

Pascal was a religious genius with a style of extraordinary distinction. He was also a great man of science, in the first rank among the *savants* of an age in which scientific knowledge was advancing with rapid strides and in which many remarkable intellects were devoting themselves to its advancement. But he was not a great philosopher; even if we look at his reflections upon the profound religious experience which he unquestionably enjoyed, it is not exactness of thought (despite the reminiscences of mathematical method which colour his language) that distinguishes them, but the tragic sense of sin, the passionate aspiration after God, the no less passionate devotion to the Redeemer to whom, as he says,[1] 'he stretches out his arms', and in communion with whom, when met and embraced, he enjoyed a like rapture of devotion to that which inspired the immortal apostrophe: [2]

> Jesu, spes poenitentibus,
> quam pius es petentibus,
> quam bonus te quaerentibus;
> sed quid invenientibus?

[1] P. § 737, p. 680.
[2] Often attributed to St. Bernard; but see F. J. E. Raby, *Christian Latin Poetry*, p. 330. Cp. R. Vaux in the *Church Quarterly Review* for April 1929, pp. 120 ff.

Console-toi, tu ne me chercherais pas si tu ne m'avais trouvé—tu ne me chercherais pas si tu ne me possédais. Ne t'inquiète donc pas. It is in these words, already quoted, which Pascal puts into the mouth of his Lord, that we find the essence and the culmination of what he has to tell us about Religion.

INDEX